THIRD TIME AROUND

THIRD TIME AROUND

*A History of the Pro-Life Movement
from the First Century to the Present*

GEORGE GRANT

Wolgemuth & Hyatt, Publishers, Inc.
Brentwood, Tennessee

The mission of Wolgemuth & Hyatt, Publishers, Inc. is to publish and distribute books that lead individuals toward:

- A personal faith in the one true God: Father, Son, and Holy Spirit;

- A lifestyle of practical discipleship; and

- A worldview that is consistent with the historic, Christian faith.

Moreover, the Company endeavors to accomplish this mission at a reasonable profit and in a manner which glorifies God and serves His Kingdom.

© 1991 by George Grant. All rights reserved.
Published January 1991. First Edition.
Printed in the United States of America.
97 96 95 94 93 92 91 90   8 7 6 5 4 3 2 1

Unless otherwise noted, all Scripture quotations are from the author's own translation.

Scripture quotations marked NKJV are from the New King James Version of the Bible, © 1979, 1980, 1982, 1984 by Thomas Nelson, Inc., Nashville, Tennessee and are used by permission.

Wolgemuth & Hyatt, Publishers, Inc.
1749 Mallory Lane, Suite 110
Brentwood, Tennessee 37027

Library of Congress Cataloging-in-Publication Data

Grant, George, 1954–
    Third time around : a history of the pro-life movement from the first century to the present / George Grant. — 1st ed.
        p. cm.
    Includes bibliographical references and index.
    ISBN 0-943497-65-5
    1. Abortion—Religious aspects—Christianity. 2. Pro-life movement—History. I. Title.
HQ767.25.G73 1991
261.8'36667'09—dc20   90-20838
                                                           CIP

To All the Faithful Through the Ages:
Who Have Had to Go Round and Round
In the Struggle for Life
Not Once, Not Twice, But Three Times

And

To My Own Beloved Children:
Who Will Have to Take Up the Cause
The Next Time Around

Dabit qui dedit

CONTENTS

ACKNOWLEDGMENTS

ost writers can truthfully say, "I hate to write, but I love having written." I know at least that *this* writer can truthfully say that.

This wasn't a book that I wanted to write. It wasn't even a book that I wanted to have written. Not only was my schedule already overcrowded and my calendar overcommitted, but my mind, will, and emotions were overextended. I certainly believed that the message of the book needed to be told, but I didn't see how I could possibly be the one to tell it. But, like Ananias, the reluctant witness of the book of Acts, I was pressed into service. The spiritual responsibility was inescapable, no matter how I squirmed or rationalized.

Thankfully, in His good providence, God provided a number of dear friends, colleagues, and yokefellows, who encouraged me along the way so that my indentured service might be joyous and not burdensome.

My friend and colleague, Mark Horne, labored faithfully with me on this project. Of all the books that I have written, this is the first one that God has afforded me the privilege of having someone help me with the research—to check facts, to dig up odd out-of-print details, and to share the vision for the work with me from start to finish. Mark did all these things and more—particularly in the "needle-in-a-haystack" research for chapter 5. Mere thanks cannot begin to convey the gratefulness I feel for his ministry in my life.

My selfless administrative assistant, Mary Jane Morris, did more than anyone—besides my wife and children, of course—to keep my life and work on an even keel during the months of writing. She managed my schedule, handled the phone, organized my library, and pumped me full of vitamins. I don't know what I would have done without her.

My pastor, Dr. D. James Kennedy, and the entire ministry staff of Coral Ridge Presbyterian Church and Knox Theological Seminary graciously supported all my efforts and endeavors both directly and indirectly by faithfully proclaiming the eternal message of our Sovereign King in word and deed. Bill Breslin, Gladys Israels, Addison Soltau, Marilyn King, Ron Kilpatrick, Gary Fallon, Wiley Stinnett, Alan Harkey, Bonnie Bunce, Rhoeda Beardsley, George Knight, Kathy Israels, and Bob Allen have been especially used by God as a provocation in my life "toward love and good works" (Hebrews 10:24–25).

My colaborers with the poor and the homeless—Barbara Gibson, Manny Sebastian, Val Parr, and Elsie D'Angelis—carried the extra burdens of ministry while I was cloistered away reading, researching, and writing. My immediate staff at Coral Ridge Ministries, Carole Sue Quarquesso, Jennifer Burkett, Charles Wolfe, Nancy Britt, and Susan Allen, worked remarkably hard in terribly unrewarding tasks—counseling clients, answering calls, scrounging details, and gofering odd tasks—while I hunkered over a keyboard. In addition, John Cochrane, Kevin Loy, Jerry and Ande Stapella, Wayne Morris, Roger Israels, Jim Brown, Vic Brudenel, Leslie Kidd, Matt and Nancy Roberts, Don and Suzanne Martin, Larry Pratt, James B. Jordan, Craig Markva, Peter Leithart, and Mac N. Tosh enabled me to do what I do by being what they are.

My dear friends in the pro-life movement all across the world have helped me immensely by checking facts, providing additional research, and making cogent criticisms. I am especially thankful to Joe Schiedler, Mercedes Wilson, Joseph Doblehoff, Roy and Sandy McKasson, Marvin and

Susan Olasky, Bishop Austin Vaughn, János and Wilma Földényi, Paul deParrie, Jack Willke, Father Paul Marx, David Shepherd, Father Gordon Walker, Angela de Malherbe, Marijo Zivkövic, Robert Whelan, Randy Terry, Jerome Lejeune, Pat Mahoney, Art Tomlinson, and Franky Schaeffer for their sacrificial efforts for the unwanted and unloved, the despised and rejected.

Despite the fact that we are living in a time and a culture where Martha Quinn's "Closet Classics" on MTV very nearly represent the limits of our historical interest, my publishers—and my dear friends—Robert Wolgemuth, Mike Hyatt, Dan Wolgemuth, and David Dunham believed in this project. Not only did they believe in it, but they also waited patiently for it past four deadlines and three catalogs. That's commitment.

My midnight serenaders—Kemper Crabb, Felix Mendelssohn, Bob Bennett, Johann Sebastian Bach, Craig Smith, Robert Schumann, Michael Card, Frederic Chopin, Dennis Welch, Franz Peter Schubert, and Ted Sandquist—soothed my soul and smoothed my path.

It is amazing how Christian *koinonia* can transform duty into joy.

Now that this project is behind me—and what needed to be said is actually said—I can affirm that I'm glad that I had to write it.

But, in all honesty, I'm even gladder to have written it.

Feast of Wenceslas
Fort Lauderdale, Florida

INTRODUCTION: ROUND AND ROUND

facta non verba [1]

Oh, to lay the bridle on the neck of Pegasus and let him go forward while in the saddle meanwhile sitting well back, gripping with the knee, taking the race, and on the energy of that steed visit the wheeling stars.

Hilaire Belloc

The fairy tale can be more sane about a seven-headed dragon than the Duchess of Somerset can be about a School Board.

G. K. Chesterton

he hot Kelvin lights bore down on us. Cameras whirred. Production personnel bustled. The host prodded and cajoled. Nervous tension filled the air like the saccharined stench of freshly machined steel.

What had already been an unpleasant enough conversation was charged with even more tension as we raced toward a conclusion. The local director of Planned Parenthood looked fiercely across the impeccable set and sallied a few final clichés and nixons. I rhetorically riposted.

In desperation as the seconds slipped away, he made one last lunging stab: "What I don't understand about you pro-lifers is where you've been all these years." The camera moved in to capture the high drama. Passion shone from his anguished features. Beads of sweat trickled down his brow. "Women have been suffering for centuries. The pro-life movement didn't even exist until 1973. You're just a bunch of extremists, opportunists, and Johnny-come-latelies."

My turn. The camera zoomed in to catch my reaction. I just smiled. "Ah, but once again, there is where you are so very wrong: The pro-life movement is not a recent phenomenon or innovation," I said. "It is two thousand years old. You see, the pro-life movement was inaugurated on a rugged old cross, on a hill called Calvary—it is best known as *Christianity*. Caring for the helpless, the deprived, and the unwanted is not simply what we *do*. It is what we *are*. Always has been. Always will be."

Cut. Break for commercial and the prerecorded outro wrap.

Stung by his obvious setback, the director of Planned Parenthood gathered up his gaggle of supporters and proponents and stormed out of the television studio. The host of the local program sauntered off to some comfortable corner to sulk and primp. And my small pro-life contingent in the audience became unusually ecstatic.

I have to say that that reaction took me by surprise.

Certainly, I wasn't surprised that my adversary was incensed. I wasn't even surprised by the cool dismissal of my host. What caught me off guard was the serendipitous reaction of my friends in the pro-life movement:

"Wow. I'd never heard *anything* like *that* before."

"Was there *really* a pro-life movement *before* 1973?"

"I didn't even know that abortion was an *issue* before Roe v. Wade."

"Where can I read about the kind of pro-life activity Christians have been involved in in the past?"

Over the next several months, as I traveled around the country—and even around the world—working with pro-life leaders from virtually every major organization, across all ecclesiastical boundaries, and in every strata of life, I was rather astonished to discover a similar unfamiliarity with our rich pro-life heritage. People who had been valiant in the battle for life were generally unaware of the fact that the battle had already been fought and won—several times—by Christian pro-life stalwarts generations, and even centuries, ago.

And I was entirely unprepared for that. After all, here we were, decades into a ferocious new life-and-death struggle over abortion, infanticide, and euthanasia—and up until now, we haven't been doing too terribly well in that struggle. So, how could we be so negligently uninformed of *our own legacy?* How could we be incognizant of such a wealth of wisdom and experience? Why does it seem like we are perpetually stuck at square one—always having to start from scratch? Why are we incessantly trying to re-invent the wheel? Why aren't we building on the successes of the past? How could it be that we are entirely oblivious to those earlier victories? Why don't we know who those ancestral pro-life heroes were, what kind of tactics they used, how they mobilized their communities, whether they worked within the system or outside it? What is it that we have been thinking about all this time? And, what have we been doing?

This book is an attempt not only to answer those questions, but also to anticipate a few new questions as well. Because of its abbreviated format, only a skeletal introduction to this vast subject is possible, but it is my hope that it will be just enough to enable us to take the first steps toward recapturing the treasure of our lost legacy.

President Harry Truman once asserted that, "The only thing that is new is the history that we don't know."[2] He was right.

≈   ≈   ≈

History is a subjective art, not a dispassionate science. As a result, the divisions of time that I have settled on—though, they are for the most part rather conventional—are confessedly chosen primarily for convenience' sake. I have measured the Patristic Era from the founding of the church to the fall of Rome in 476, and I have measured the Medieval Era from the end of the empire in the West to the fall of Constantinople in 1453—which also was the year the Hundred Years War between England and France ended. The Renaissance and Enlightenment is noted from the dawning of the sixteenth century to the beginning of the French Revolution in 1789; the Missions Movement, from the dawning of the nineteenth century to the outbreak of hostilities during the Great War in 1914. And I have measured the modern era from the beginning of the twentieth century to the present. Of course, these broad brush strokes overly simplify the remarkably complex journey of men and civilizations through the ages, but they will have to do for our limited purposes here.

Legends, fables, and apocryphal stories abound in any history—and church history is certainly not an exception. Thus, finding uncontested and fully documented sources has proven to be a daunting exercise. Early on in the project, I determined to steer a middle course between academic skepticism and wide-eyed hagiography by accepting only canonical or consensus accounts of the lives and activities of pro-life heroes.

Only direct quotations are cited in the endnotes. However, a bibliography has been supplied for those readers who wish to go back to some of the original sources that I relied on for this survey. It is my hope, in fact, that this book will serve as a prod for many to explore the inestimable riches of our past.

æ   æ   æ

The English author and lecturer, John H. Y. Briggs, has poignantly argued that an historical awareness is essential for the health and well-being of any society; it enables us to know who we are, why we are here, and what we should do. He says:

Just as a loss of memory in an individual is a psychiatric defect calling for medical treatment, so too any community which has no social memory is suffering from an illness.[3]

Lord Acton, the great historian from the previous generation, made the same point saying:

History must be our deliverer not only from the undue influence of other times, but from the undue influence of our own, from the tyranny of the environment and the pressures of the air we breathe.[4]

This book—which I admit with chagrined irony had its genesis on a live television program—is offered as a humble beginning to what I pray may be an historical corrective. It is offered so that we may indeed recover from our present illness and escape our present tyranny.

Deo soli gloria. Jesu juva.

PART 1

THE FIRST TIME AROUND

Time after time mankind is driven against the rocks of the horrid reality of a fallen creation. And time after time mankind must learn the hard lessons of history—the lessons that for some dangerous and awful reason we can't seem to keep in our collective memory.
Hilaire Belloc

Weak things must boast of being new, like so many new German philosophies. But strong things can boast of being old. Strong things can boast of being moribund.
G. K. Chesterton

IN THE VALLEY OF THE SHADOW OF DEATH: AN ANTHROPOLOGY

abyssus abssum invocat [1]

> *There is no fortress of man's flesh so made, but subtle, treacherous time comes creeping in. Oh, long before his last assaults begin, the enemy's on; the stronghold is betrayed; and the one lonely watchman, half-dismayed, beyond the covering of dark, he hears them come: the distant hosts of death that march with muffled drum.*

> Hilaire Belloc

> *There is above all this supreme stamp of the barbarian; the sacrifice of the permanent to the temporary.*

> G. K. Chesterton

he hue and cry arose to heaven. Raw passion gripped men and women alike. Dark with human frailty, the architecture of their souls scuttled them from one extreme to another: from wailing grief to insane murmuring, from desperate hilarity to catatonic shock, from enraged cursing to soft choking sobs.[2]

Broken bodies. Cast-off lives. Stark-naked tragedy. Gore and devastation. Sadness and sorrow. There before them was the vexing spector of mortality and the awful stench of

death. It was a gruesome panorama that defiled their
senses and haunted their every waking thought.

It was a nightmare come to life.

The carnage was beyond their comprehension. The loss
was beyond their measure. But the memory of it would be
carved onto the fleshly tablets of their hearts with a dull,
familiar blade.

It was an all too recognizable scene—it still is.

It could describe for us the savage anguish of Israelite
mothers after Pharaoh ordered the deaths of all their male
children (see Exodus 1:15–22). It could describe for us the
desperate terror that raged through Gilead after the ma-
rauding army of Ammon ripped open their pregnant
women and raped their daughters (see Amos 1:13–15). It
could describe for us the dreadful pall that gripped the families of Bethlehem after Herod slaughtered all their infant
sons in a fit of jealousy (see Matthew 2:16–18). Or, it could
describe for us any one of thousands of other vignettes that
litter our cultural subconscious like parched bones in the
howling wilderness—from the ovens of Auschwitz to the
gulags of Siberia, from the prisons of Teheran to the streets
of Beirut, from the hospitals of Bloomington to the
aborturaries of New York.

Indeed, such tragedy is a well-worn human landscape.
Such calamity clutters the pages of human history. Such
pathos persistently torments the hodge-podge ideals of
human hope. Replayed again and again and again, it has
become a semiotic symbol of the end of man and the end
of his doing.

Like a moth drawn to a candle flame, man deals in
death. He always has. He always will. For that is his nature
in this poor fallen world.

The Thanatos Factor

Sadly, because all men without exception are sinners, the
most fundamental factor in understanding anthropology

(the study of men) is the *thanatos* factor. With entirely non-Freudian implications, the *thanatos* syndrome is simply the natural sinful inclination to death and defilement. All men have morbidly embraced death (see Romans 5:12).

At the Fall, mankind was suddenly destined for death (see Jeremiah 15:2). We were all at that moment bound into a covenant with death (see Isaiah 28:15). Scripture tells us, "There is a way that seems right to a man, but its end is the way of death" (Proverbs 14:12; 16:25, NKJV).

Whether we know it or not, we have chosen death (see Jeremiah 8:3). It has become our shepherd (see Psalm 49:14). Our minds are fixed on it (see Romans 8:6), our hearts pursue it (see Proverbs 21:6), and our flesh is ruled by it (see Romans 8:2). We dance to its cadences (see Proverbs 2:18) and descend to its chambers (see Proverbs 7:27).

The fact is, "the wages of sin is death" (Romans 6:23, NKJV) and "all have sinned" (Romans 3:23, NKJV).

> There is none righteous, not even one; there is none who understands, there is none who seeks for God; all have turned aside, together they have become useless; there is none who does good, there is not even one. Their throat is an open grave, with their tongues they keep deceiving, the poison of asps is under their lips; whose mouth is full of cursing and bitterness; their feet are swift to shed blood, destruction and misery are in their paths, and the path of peace have they not known. There is no fear of God before their eyes. (Romans 3:10–18)
>
> And, all those who hate God, love death. (Proverbs 8:36)

It is no wonder then that abortion, infanticide, exposure, and abandonment have always been a normal and natural part of human relations. Since the dawning of time, men have contrived ingenious diversions to satisfy their fallen passions. And child-killing has always been chief among them.

Virtually every culture in antiquity was stained with the blood of innocent children. Unwanted infants in ancient Rome were abandoned outside the city walls to die from exposure to the elements or from the attacks of wild foraging beasts. Greeks often gave their pregnant women harsh doses of herbal or medicinal abortifacients. Persians developed highly sophisticated surgical curette procedures. Chinese women tied heavy ropes around their waists so excruciatingly tight that they either aborted or passed into unconsciousness. Ancient Hindus and Arabs concocted chemical pessaries—abortifacients that were pushed or pumped directly into the womb through the birth canal. Primitive Canaanites threw their children onto great flaming pyres as a sacrifice to their god Molech. Polynesians subjected their pregnant women to onerous tortures—their abdomens beaten with large stones or hot coals heaped upon their bodies. Japanese women straddled boiling cauldrons of parricidal brews. Egyptians disposed of their unwanted children by disemboweling and dismembering them shortly after birth—their collagen was then ritually harvested for the manufacture of cosmetic creams.

None of the great minds of the ancient world—from Plato and Aristotle to Seneca and Quintilian, from Pythagoras and Aristophanes to Livy and Cicero, from Herodotus and Thucydides to Plutarch and Euripides—disparaged child-killing in any way. In fact, most of them actually recommended it. They callously discussed its various methods and procedures. They casually debated its sundry legal ramifications. They blithely tossed lives like dice.

Abortion, infanticide, exposure, and abandonment were so much a part of human societies that they provided the primary *liet motif* in popular traditions, stories, myths, fables, and legends.

The founding of Rome was, for instance, presumed to be the happy result of the abandonment of children. According to the story, a vestal virgin who had been raped bore twin sons, Romulus and Remus. The harsh Etruscan monarch Amulius ordered them exposed on the Tiber River. Left in a basket which floated ashore, they were found by a she-wolf and suckled by her. Later, a shepherd discovered them and took them home to his wife, and the kindly couple brought them up as their own. Romulus and Remus would later establish the city of Rome on the seven hills near the place of their rescue.

Oedipus was presumed to be an abandoned child who was also found by a shepherd and later rose to greatness. Ion, the eponymous monarch in ancient Greece miraculously lived through an abortion, according to tradition. Cyrus, the founder of the Persian empire, was supposedly a fortunate survivor of infanticide. According to Homer's legend, Paris, whose amorous indiscretions started the Trojan War, was also a victim of abandonment. Telephus, the king of Mysia in Greece, and Habius, ruler of the Cunetes in Spain, had both been exposed as children according to various folk tales. Jupiter, chief god of the Olympian pantheon, himself had been abandoned as a child. He in turn exposed his twin sons, Zethus and Amphion. Similarly, other myths related that Poseidon, Aesculapius, Hephaistos, Attis, and Cybele had all been abandoned to die.

Because they had been mired by the minions of sin and death, it was as natural as the spring rains for the men and women of antiquity to kill their children. It was as instinctive as the autumn harvest for them to summarily sabotage their own heritage. They saw nothing particularly cruel about despoiling the fruit of their wombs. It was woven into the very fabric of their culture. They believed that it was completely justifiable. They believed that it was just and good and right.

But they were wrong. Dreadfully wrong.

The Life of the World

Life is God's gift. It is His gracious endowment upon the created order. It flows forth in generative fruitfulness. The earth is literally *teeming* with life (see Genesis 1:20; Leviticus 11:10; 22:5; Deuteronomy 14:9). And the crowning glory of this sacred teeming is man himself (see Genesis 1:26–30; Psalm 8:1–9). To violate the sanctity of this magnificent endowment is to fly in the face of all that is holy, just, and true (see Jeremiah 8:1–17; Romans 8:6).

To violate the sanctity of life is to invite judgment, retribution, and anathema (see Deuteronomy 30:19–20). It is to solicit devastation, imprecatation, and destruction (see Jeremiah 21:8–10). The Apostle Paul tells us, "Do not be deceived, God is not mocked, whatsoever a man sows, that he shall also reap" (Galatians 6:7).

But the Lord God, who is the giver of life (see Acts 17:25), the fountain of life (see Psalm 36:9), the defender of life (see Psalm 27:1), the prince of life (see Acts 3:15), and the restorer of life (see Ruth 4:15), did not leave men to languish hopelessly in the clutches of sin and death. He not only sent us the message of life (see Acts 5:20) and the words of life (see John 6:68), He sent us the light of life as well (see John 8:12). He sent us His only begotten Son— the life of the world (see John 6:51)—to break the bonds of death (see 1 Corinthians 15:54–56). Jesus "tasted death for everyone" (Hebrews 2:9), actually abolishing death for our sakes (see 2 Timothy 1:10) and offering us new life (see John 5:21).

> For God so loved the world, that He sent His only begotten Son, that whosoever believeth in Him should not perish, but have everlasting life. (John 3:16, KJV)

One of the earliest Christian documents—actually predating much of the New Testament—asserts that "There are two ways: a way of life and a way of death."[3] In Christ, God has afforded us the opportunity to choose between those two ways—to choose between fruitful and teeming life on the one hand, and barren and impoverished death on the other (see Deuteronomy 30:19).

Apart from Christ it is not possible to escape the snares of sin and death (see Colossians 2:13). On the other hand, "If any man be in Christ, he is a new creation; old things have passed away; behold, all things have become new" (2 Corinthians 5:17).

All those who hate Christ "love death" (Proverbs 8:36); while all those who receive Christ are made the sweet savor of life (see 2 Corinthians 2:16).

The implication is clear: The pro-life movement and the Christian faith are synonymous. Where there is one, there will be the other—for one cannot be had without the other.

Further, the primary conflict in temporal history always has been and always will be the struggle for life by the church against the natural inclinations of all men everywhere.

Conclusion

Death has cast its dark shadow across the whole of human relations. Because of sin, all men flirt and flaunt shamelessly in the face of its spector. Sadly, such impudence has led to the most grotesque concupiscence imaginable: the slaughter of innocent children. Blinded by the glare from the nefarious and insidious angel of light (see 2 Corinthians 11:14), we stand by, paralyzed and mesmerized.

Thanks be to God, there is a way of escape from these bonds of destruction. In Christ, there is hope. In Him there is life, both temporal and eternal. In Him there is liberty and justice. In Him there is an antidote to the *thanatos* factor. In Him, and in Him alone, there is an answer to the age-long dilemma of the dominion of death.

HOW FIRM
A FOUNDATION:
THE APOSTOLIC CHURCH

a maximis ad minima [1]

Faith begins to make one abandon the old way of judging. Averages and movements and the rest grow uncertain. The very nature of social force seems changed to us. And this is hard when a man has loved common views.

Hilaire Belloc

Faith is always at a disadvantage; it is a perpetually defeated thing which survives all conquerors.

G. K. Chesterton

t was into a family of great wealth and distinction that Basil of Caesarea was born midway through the fourth century. Of all the great dynasties that mankind has seen emerge out of the sea of convention and commonality, perhaps none has left as permanent an impress on the course of history as that of the Cappadocian Valenzias.[2] The Habsburgs, the Romanovs, and the Medicis were prodigious in their accomplishments. The Stuarts, the Bourbons, and the Mings were remarkable for their impact. The Warburgs, the Rothschilds, and the Carlyles gave shape to one generation after another. But, the Valenzias outshone them all.

Basil's grandmother, Macri of Lyyra; his father, Battia of Cappadocia; his mother, Emmelia of Athens; his sister, Macrina of Pontus; and his two younger brothers, Gregory of Nyssa and Peter of Sebastea, were all numbered among the early saints of the church. One of his other brothers, Paulus of Ry, became Chief Counsel to the Emperor and still another, Stephen of Alexandria, became the Imperial Governor of Byzantium's largest colonial region. Three of his descendents eventually bore the Imperial Scepter and two others ascended to the ecumenical throne. For more than a thousand years some member of this remarkable family held a high position in Constantinople's corridors of power and influence.

But as great as his family was, Basil was himself greater still.

Renowned for his encyclopedic learning, he studied in all the great schools of his day—in Caesarea, Constantinople, Athens, and Rome. For a short time he practiced law with an eye toward a public career, but he determined to heed a call into the ministry instead. He helped to establish a Christian community in Annesi where he distinguished himself as a man of extraordinary charity and brilliance. It was not long before his reputation reached the farthest edges of the Empire: He was a quick-witted adversary to the heretical Arians; he was a valiant defender of orthodoxy; he had a productive theological pen; and he was a man who combined a deep and sincere piety with a tough and realistic practicality. In short order, he was called to the very prominent parish ministry of Caesarea.

Diligent to perform his pastoral duties, Basil soon found himself overwhelmed with busyness. He led eighteen services every week—except just before Christmas and Easter when there were more—in addition to his work of catechizing the young, visiting the sick, and encouraging the distressed. He also kept up a heavy correspondence and continued his theological output. Despite all this, he was able to involve himself in the issues and concerns of the day. He was deeply moved by the plight of the poor and spent his life seeking practical ways to alleviate their suffering and to facilitate their recovery. He instituted the practice of almsgiving in Caesarea, utilizing the resources of the church in order to create new opportunities for the needy, in order to transform their poverty into productivity. Because health care is an important part of that process—and because the poor were generally denied access to anything but the crassest form of folk medicine—Basil opened the very first non-ambulatory hospital.

It was his involvement with the poor and his work in the hospital that ultimately led Basil into a confrontation with still another series of societal woes: abortion, infanticide, exposure, and abandonment. Despite the fact that Christianity had obtained official status some forty years earlier, the Cappadocian region was not yet thoroughly evangelized and a number of pagan practices persisted, including noxious child-killing.

Basil was horrified.

He discovered a guild of abortionists, or *sagae*, that were doing a booming trade in Caesarea and the surrounding environs. They provided herbal potions, pessaries, and even surgical remedies for women who wished to avoid child-bearing. The bodies of the children were then harvested and sold to cosmetologists in Egypt, who used the collagen for the manufacture of various beauty creams.

When Basil approached several city officials about the horrors that the *sagae* were perpetrating on the women and children of the community, he was shocked to discover that the awful trade was perfectly legal—and always had been.

Immediately, he sprang into action: He preached a series of sermons on the sanctity of human life; he mobilized the members of his church to help care for families and women who were facing crisis pregnancies; he began to exercise the full weight of his family influence as well as his own considerable powers of persuasion to change the laws; he began an education program throughout the entire city so that people could fully understand the issues; he took imprecatory ecclesiastical action against the *sagae*, declaring them to be anathema; and he even staged public protests against the Egyptian traders that helped to support the grisly trade with their mercantile ingenuity.

Basil was unequivocal in his advocacy of life. He wrote:

> She who has deliberately destroyed a fetus must bear the penalty for murder. Moreover those who aid her, who give abortifacients for the destruction of a child con-ceived in the womb are murderers themselves, along with those receiving the poisons.[3]

But, that was by no means the end of the matter. A precedent as legitimately tenured and as deeply rooted as child-killing would not be easily dispatched.

According to the centuries old tradition of *paterfamilias*, the birth of a Roman was not a biological fact. Infants were received into the world only as the family willed. A Roman did not *have* a child; he *took* a child. Immediately after birthing, if the family decided not to *raise* the child—liter-ally, lifting him above the earth—he was simply aban-doned. There were special high places or walls outside most Roman cities where the newborn was taken and ex-posed to die.

Basil had heard of exposure, but he was amazed to dis-cover that it too was still perfectly legal—and was, at least to some limited degree, still practiced. So, he broadened his pro-life attentions, not only opposing the *sagae*, but also lobbying to have *paterfamilias* abrogated, the exposure walls decimated, and the high places brought down.

So passionate was Basil in his concern for life that ap-parently, late one evening after Vespers, he and several deacons from the church actually went outside the city to dismantle the old Caesarean infanticide shrine with their bare hands. He knew that such direct action could very well have jeopardized his standing, but he was driven by an irrepressible spiritual imperative.

Hearing of Basil's solitary crusade, the Emperor Valentinian took the first step toward the full criminalization of child-killing in 374 by decreeing, "All parents must support their children conceived; those who brutalize or abandon them should be subject to the full penalty prescribed by law."[4]

For the first time in human history, abortion, infanticide, exposure, and abandonment were made illegitimate. The *sagae* were driven underground and eventually out of business altogether. The tradition of *paterfamilias* was all but overturned. The exposure walls were destroyed. And the high places were brought low.

When Basil died just four years later at the age of fifty, he had not only made his mark on the church, he had also altered the course of human history—and he had laid the groundwork for the flowering of one of the greatest family dynasties mankind has ever known.

The Biblical Mandate

Basil's commitment to protecting innocent life was not rooted simply in a personal preference or prejudice. He did not subjectively pull his view of the sanctity of life out of thin air. Instead, it was an obedient response to God's own revelation: the Bible.

It was abundantly clear to him that the Scriptures commanded a reverence for life. Embedded in every book and interwoven into every doctrine was the unwavering standard of justice and mercy for all: the weak and the strong, the great and the small, the rich and the poor, the lame and the whole, the young and the old, and the born and the unborn.

The Bible declares the sanctity of life in its account of God's *creation* (see Genesis 1:26–28; Psalm 36:9; Psalm 104:24–30; John 1:3–4; Acts 17:25; 1 Timothy 6:13).

Woe to him who strives with his Maker! Let the potsherd strive with the potsherds of the earth. Shall the clay say to him who forms it, "What are you making?" Or shall your handiwork say, "He has no hands"? Woe to him who says to his father, "What are you begetting?" Or to the woman, "What have you brought forth?" Thus says the LORD, the Holy One of Israel, and his Maker: "Ask Me of things to come concerning My sons; and concerning the work of My hands, you command Me. I have made the earth, and created man on it. It was my hands that stretched out the heavens, and all their host I have commanded. (Isaiah 45:9–12, NKJV)

The Bible declares the sanctity of life in its description of God's *sovereignty* (see Deuteronomy 32:39; Job 10:12; Psalm 22:9–10; John 5:21; Romans 11:36; Colossians 1:16–17).

For You have formed my inward parts; You have covered me in my mother's womb. I will praise You, for I am fearfully and wonderfully made; marvelous are Your works, and that my soul knows very well. My frame was not hidden from you, when I was made in secret, and skillfully wrought in the lowest parts of the earth. Your eyes saw my substance, being yet unformed. And in Your Book they all were written, the days fashioned for me, when as yet there were none of them. (Psalm 139:13–16, NKJV)

The Bible declares the sanctity of life in its discussion of the *incarnation* (see John 3:16; John 11:25; John 14:6; Acts 2:22–28; Romans 5:21; Colossians 3:4).

The thief does not come except to steal, and to kill, and to destroy. I have come that they may have life, and that they may have it more abundantly. (John 10:10, NKJV)

The Bible declares the sanctity of life in its explanation of Christ's *redemption* (see Matthew 18:10–11; Mark 10:45; Romans 8:11; 1 Corinthians 2:16; 1 John 5:11–12).

But has now been revealed by the appearing of our Savior Jesus Christ, who has abolished death and brought life and immortality to light through the gospel. (2 Timothy 1:10, NKJV)

The Bible declares the sanctity of life in its exposition of ethical *justice* (see Genesis 9:6; Exodus 20:13; Exodus 21:22–25; Leviticus 24:17; Isaiah 1:15; 1 Peter 3:7).

> I call heaven and earth as witnesses today against you, that I have set before you life and death, blessing and cursing; therefore choose life, that both you and your descendants may live. (Deuteronomy 30:19, NKJV)

The Bible declares the sanctity of life in its exhortation to covenantal *mercy* (see Deuteronomy 10:18; Isaiah 1:17; Isaiah 58:6–7; Acts 5:20; Titus 2:11–14; James 1:27).

> If you faint in the day of adversity, your strength is small. Deliver those who are drawn toward death, and hold back those stumbling to the slaughter. If you say, "Surely we did not know this," does not He who weighs the heart consider it? He who keeps your soul, does He not know it? (Proverbs 24:10–12a, NKJV)

From Genesis to Revelation (see Genesis 2:7; Revelation 22:17), in the books of the Law (see Exodus 4:12; Leviticus 19:16), in the books of history (see Judges 13:2–24; 1 Samuel 16:7), in the books of wisdom (see Psalm 68:5–6; Proverbs 29:7), in the prophetic books (see Amos 1:13; Jeremiah 1:5), in the Gospels (see Matthew 10:31; Luke 1:15, 41–44), and in the epistles (see Galatians 1:15; 1 Corinthians 15:22), the pro-life message of the Bible is absolutely inescapable.

It was this "Word of Life" (Philippians 2:16) that Basil had believed—and it was this Word that he acted on faithfully.

The Consensus of the Church

Basil was not alone in his affirmation of the Biblical message of life or in his condemnation of child-killing. In fact, the wholehearted consensus of the Apostolic Era was that all life was a sacred gift from God and that any breach of that gift was nothing less than murder. There were no *ifs, ands,* or *buts* about it. On that, all of the patristics absolutely agreed.

The *Didache* was a compilation of Apostolic moral teachings that appeared at the end of the first century. Among its many admonitions, it asserted an unwavering reverence for the sanctity of life:

> There are two ways: the way of life and the way of death, and the difference between these two ways is great. Therefore, do not murder a child by abortion or kill a newborn infant.[5]

The *Epistle of Barnabas* was an early second century theological tract that was highly regarded by the first Christian communities. Like the *Didache*, it laid down absolute strictures against abortion and infanticide:

> You shall love your neighbor more than your own life. You shall not slay a child by abortion. You shall not kill that which has already been generated.[6]

The second century judicial theorist and Christian apologist Athenagoras, in a letter to Emperor Marcus Aurelius, wrote:

> We say that women who induce abortions are murderers, and will have to give account of it to God. The fetus in the womb is a living being and therefore the object of God's care.[7]

In the third century, the sage pastor and theologian, Clement of Alexandria, asserted that:

> Our whole life can proceed according to God's perfect plan only if we gain dominion over our desires, practicing continence from the beginning instead of destroying through perverse and pernicious arts human offspring, who are given birth by Divine Providence. Those who

use abortifacient medicines to hide their fornication cause not only the outright murder of the fetus but of the whole human race as well.[8]

At about the same time, the brilliant and prolific Tertullian composed his *Apology*. There he connected the sanctity of life with the very integrity of the gospel:

> Our faith declares life out of death. Therefore, murder is forbidden once and for all. We may not destroy even the fetus in the womb. To hinder a birth is merely a speedier man killing. Thus it does not matter whether you take away a life that is born, or destroy one that is coming to the birth. In both instances, destruction is murder.[9]

Ambrose, the renowned and revered bishop of Milan, was forthright in his condemnation of those engaged in child-killing procedures:

> They deny in their very womb their own progeny. By use of parricidal mixtures they snuff out the fruit of their wombs. In this way life is taken before it is given. Who except man himself has taught us ways of repudiating our own children.[10]

Similarly, the great Latin scholar and ecclesiastic, Jerome, added his voice of protest:

> They who drink potions to ensure sterility are guilty of rebuffing God's own blessings. Some, when they learn that the potions have failed and thus are with child through sin, practice abortion by use of still other potions. They are then guilty of three crimes: self-mutilation, adultery, and the murder of an unborn child.[11]

Augustine, august bishop of Hippo, condemned those whose "lustful cruelty" drove them to extremes:

> They provoke women to such extravagant methods as to use poisonous drugs to secure barrenness; or else, if unsuccessful in this, to murder the unborn child.[12]

Any survey of the life and teaching of the early church reveals the fact that the patristics translated the Biblical injunction to protect the sanctity of life into their life and doctrine.

Word and Deed

The pro-life position of the early church was not mere dogma. The patristics matched their rhetoric with reality. They worked hard and sacrificed dearly for the sake of life.

In Rome, Christians rescued babies that had been abandoned on the exposure walls outside the city—often illegally and at great risk to themselves. These *foundlings* would then be adopted and raised up in the nurture and admonition of the Lord.

In Corinth, Christians offered charity, mercy, and refuge to temple prostitutes who had become pregnant—again, standing against the tide of community expectations. These despised and exploited women were taken into homes where they could safely have their children and then get a fresh start on life.

In Poitiers, Christians cared for the poor, the sick, and the lame in clinics and hostels. The church sacrificed its own personal peace and affluence by protecting and providing for those unwanted and dispossessed souls without partiality.

Clearly, Christians were not simply *against* child-killing. They were *for* life. Whenever and wherever the gospel went out, believers emphasized the priority of good works, especially works of compassion toward the needy. For the first time in human history, hospitals were founded, orphanages were established, rescue missions were started, almshouses were built, soup kitchens were begun, shelters were endowed, charitable societies were incorporated, and relief agencies were commissioned. The hungry were fed; the naked, clothed; the homeless, sheltered; the sick, nursed;

the aged, honored; the unborn, protected; and the handicapped, cherished.

The heroes of the faith who demonstrated the grace of Christ through such deeds of kindness during the apostolic era were legion:

- *Addai of Edessa* was one of the Apostle Thomas's earliest disciples. Sometime at the end of the first century he was sent to what is now Urfa in Iraq. There he established the church and launched innumerable evangelistic enterprises. He also was forced to confront the barbarous program of child limitation and elimination practiced in that region. Eventually, he was martyred for his refusal to temper his pro-life fulminations.

- *Benignus of Dijon* was a missionary from Lyons who was martyred in Epagny in the late second century. He was renowned for his generosity and charity especially to the sick and suffering. A mob of superstitious citizens in that pre-Christian Gallic region slew him because he nursed, supported, and protected a number of deformed and crippled children that had been saved from death after failed abortions or exposures.

- *Callistus of Rome* was a Christian slave who was imprisoned and sentenced to hard labor in the Sardinian quarries late in the second century after becoming involved in a scandalous financial scheme. After his release he was emancipated and put in charge of the church's shelter and cemetery on the Appian Way which still bears his name. He faithfully occupied himself with his duties—caring for the poor, comforting the bereaved, and giving refuge to the dispossessed. His compassion for abandoned children was especially noteworthy—it was Callistus that helped to organize the famed "Life Watches" that placed hundreds of exposed children into Christian homes. Eventually, he was chosen to serve as Bishop of Rome.

- *Alban of Verlamium* is widely venerated as the first Christian martyr on the island of Britain. During the last few

decades of the second century he offered refuge to
those fleeing the persecution against the church. He
succored the sick, cared for the poor, and saved abandoned children from certain death. Bede the historian
records his brutal martyrdom on Holmhurst Hill after
he tried to intercede on behalf of a pitiful family of
refugees.

- Late in the third century, *Afra of Augsburg* developed a
  ministry to the abandoned children of prisoners,
  thieves, smugglers, pirates, runaway slaves, and brig-
  ands. Herself a former prostitute, she cared for the despised and the rejected with a special fervor, taking
  them into her home, creating an adoption network,
  and sacrificing all she had—that out of her lack they
  might be satisfied. Ultimately, her work came under
  the scrutiny of the authorities, and she was martyred
  during the great persecution of Diocletian.

- *George of Diospolis,* patron of both England and Leba-
  non, was a Christian soldier who gained fame after several daring rescues of children in distress. He was
  known as the "Dragonslayer," not so much because of
  exploits with rare and dangerous reptiles, but because
  of his willingness to snatch innocent life out of the jaws
  of death. Eventually, he too fell victim to Diocletian's
  wrath in the persecution of 304, and was beheaded in
  Nicomedia. Later, innumerable legends made much of
  his exploits—romantically associating him with damsels
  and dragons—but it was his willingness to risk all for
  the sake of the sanctity of life that earned him his place
  in history.

- *Barlaam of Antioch* was a cobbler for the imperial forces
  who devoted all his free time to the care of orphans
  and widows in his church. Because he himself had been
  saved from the infanticide wall outside the city, he was
  especially concerned for exposed children. Even
  though he was not a pastor or church leader, his good
  deeds were so widely known that the enemies of the
  faith sought to have his witness silenced. During the

calamitous persecution in 304, they succeeded in having him martyred.

- *Telemachus of Laddia* was a monk from Syria who, while on a pilgrimage to Rome, launched a crusade to put an end to gladiatorial contests. One day during the winter of 399, after many months of fruitless lobbying, he rushed into the great arena of the Colosseum to separate the bloody combatants. The infuriated spectators mobbed him, and he died in the crush. Even so, his sacrifice was not for naught: horrified by the story of the courageous defender of life, the Emperor Honorius abolished all such contests throughout the empire.

- *Fabiola Fabii* was a wealthy member of a prominent patrician family who after a scandalous life was converted in middle age and then devoted the rest of her days to good deeds. Together with Pammachius of Bethlehem, she channeled her vast resources into the establishment of a large hospice for sick and needy travelers in Porto. It was the first institution of its kind and was widely heralded for its unbending pro-life convictions. She died in the plague of 399.

- *Nicholas of Myra,* the fourth century pastor who inspired the tradition of Santa Claus, may not have lived at the North Pole or traveled by reindeer and sleigh, but he certainly was a paradigm of graciousness, generosity, and Christian charity. His great love and concern for children drew him into a crusade that ultimately resulted in imperial pro-life statutes that remained in place in Byzantium for more than a thousand years.

In addition to these pro-life heroes of the faith, hundreds of other patristic Christians demonstrated beyond any shadow of a doubt that the doctrine of the sanctity of life was inseparable from their gospel profession: Thecla of Iconium (d. 70), Tartian of Lorrai (d. 189), Barbara of Tuscany (d. 235), Cyprian of Carthage (d. 258), Empress Helen of Drepanum (d. 330), Antony of Egypt (d. 356), Hilary of Poitiers (d. 367), Athanasius of Alexandria (d.

373), Cyril of Jerusalem (d. 386), Gregory of Nyssa (d. 395), and John Chrysostom (d. 407).

The pro-life message of the early church was a lifestyle. It was a commitment. It was a worldview. And, as a result, it made a deep and lasting impression on the whole civilized world. The minions of death were at last shaken from their tenure in the bastions of power and prestige. Even in those regions where the Christian faith never fully predominated, or where the gospel took root only to be supplanted later, the sanctity of life was grafted into the cultural conscience. Laws were changed. Traditions were uprooted. And lives were saved.

Conclusion

The early church was pro-life. They issued pro-life pronouncements. They launched pro-life activities. And they lived pro-life lifestyles. In both word and deed, they built their witness to the world around five fundamental pro-life principles:

Orthodoxy

The pioneer believers were rooted in the orthodox understanding that the creator God was, is, and ever shall be sovereign. Christ's lordship—as it is revealed in the Bible—was the starting place for all of their activity both individual and corporate. They were rooted in the Scriptures and in the marvelous orthodox heritage of those who had gone on before them: forefathers, fathers, patriarchs, prophets, apostles, preachers, evangelists, martyrs, confessors, ascetics, and every righteous spirit made perfect in faith. Thus, the early church's pro-life activity did not spring out of mere sentimental preference or uninformed prejudice. Instead, the unwavering commitment to the ethic of life was the direct result of a commitment to the Word of Life graciously given by the Lord of Life.

The Church

The early disciples recognized that the church is not only the nursery of the kingdom, but that it is the wellspring of life as well. All their activities on behalf of the innocent and helpless were part and parcel with their sacramental life of discipleship, fellowship, and worship. In practical terms, this meant that they were able to remain unified on all of the essentials. Though there was great diversity among them, the first Christians maintained a remarkable unanimity on matters of essence and substance. Their unified opposition to child-killing was unwaveringly and entirely unquestioned.

Servanthood

The message of the gospel is not a message of raw judicial power. It is a message of sacrificial grace. Jesus came as an obedient servant, not as a tyrannical overlord. He came to serve, not to subdue. And the disciples that He called to Himself were rooted in this same covenantal ethic. Thus, the early Christians not only valiantly stood *against* the tide of abortion, infanticide, abandonment, and exposure; they stood *with* the victims of brutality. To them, to be pro-life meant not only exposing the evil deeds of manipulators and oppressors; it also meant sheltering the suffering, caring for the homeless, and giving refuge to the unwanted. They self-consciously lived lives of service, compassion, and charity.

Urgency

Many of the heroes of the apostolic era jeopardized their reputations, sacrificed their well-being, and risked their lives for the sake of the weak and helpless. Their firm belief in the ultimate and consummate judgment of God drove them to follow the dictates of the faith at all costs. Thus, they rescued the perishing, confronted injustice, and

tore down the high places. Compelled by the severe urgency of child-killing and the covenantal exigency of the
gospel, they did whatever was within their capacity to do in
order for justice and truth to prevail.

Patience

Knowing that the struggle for life would not be won in a
day, the early Christians worked hard, educated their children,. involved themselves in their culture, lobbied their
magistrates, and built for the future. They knew that theirs
was a multi-generational task. And so, they laid the groundwork for a multi-generational victory. The pro-life ethic was
not an isolated single-interest issue for them. It was inte-
grated into a comprehensive covenantal worldview that
touched every area of life. Out of the context of this
worldview, they educated the people that they lived with,
worked with, worshiped with, and played with. Relying on
the promises of God, they unleashed the truth that would
ultimately set all men free.

ೂ   ೂ   ೂ

They did all this and more because, according to the
gospel, all those who walk the path of life (see Psalm 16:11;
Proverbs 2:19; 5:6; 10:17; 15:24), and eat from wisdom's
tree of life (see Proverbs 3:18; 3:22; 4:13; 4:22–23), are
made the champions of life (see Proverbs 24:10–12).

A NEW CONSENSUS:
THE MEDIEVAL CHURCH

ab ovo usque ad mala [1]

There falls on us the peaceful weight of millennium, just as the years fell upon Charlemagne in the tower of Saragosa when the battle was done; after he had curbed the valley of Ebro and christened Bramimonde.

Hilaire Belloc

They were in later times bracketed in glory, because they were in their own time bracketed in infamy; or at least in unpopularity. For they did the most unpopular thing men can do; they started a popular movement.

G. K. Chesterton

aught between two worlds—the world of a frighteningly dark primordial barbarism and the world of a bright hopeful Christian civilization— Dympna Caelrhynn was born the eldest daughter of the heathen Celtic prince, Eadburh. When she was still just a child, her beloved Christian mother was claimed by a plague. Apparently stricken mad with grief, Eadburh conceived a perverted passion for his daughter. In order to escape his incestuous intentions, she fled abroad with her chaplain Gerebernus, first to the newly Christianized port city of Antwerp, and then to the small village of Gheel about twenty-five miles away. There she began to rebuild a life for herself.

With the help of Gerebernus, she devoted herself to the care of the needy and the forlorn. She rescued dozens of orphaned children from a life of begging in the streets. She gave shelter to the lame, the mentally impaired, and the infirm. She fearlessly lobbied for justice for the poor. And she fought to expose the dark secrets of abortionists whose flourishing contraband was wreaking havoc among the peasantry.

There in the Flemish lowlands, abortion, infanticide, abandonment, and exposure were already beginning to fall out of favor as forms of family limitation. Medievalism was progressively making its mark. The gospel had permeated the culture just enough that the people had vaguely begun to recognize the fact that, as the psalmist proclaimed, "Children are an heritage of the Lord; and the fruit of the womb is a reward from Him" (Psalm 127:3).

As a result, many of the most insidious practices from antiquity were passing from the scene. Even so, when there were serious problems with a pregnancy or when handicapped children were born, in desperation many families reverted to the pagan practices.

Dympna boldly challenged this, arguing that if human life is sacred, then *all* human life must be protected. She sought to demonstrate that there was no such thing as an unwanted child. She said:

> All the starry hosts of heaven and of earth declare with one voice the glory bestowed on these sublime creatures of the Living God, these creatures made just a little lower than Himself. We can do no better than to acknowledge our acceptance of Him by our acceptance of them.[2]

Indeed, she acknowledged her love of Christ by making her home a haven for the otherwise unwanted. In the span of just three years, her household grew to include more than forty handicapped children and another twenty mentally impaired adolescents and adults.

Before long, she had gained a remarkable reputation for selflessness, graciousness, and charity. In the trying times of the early eighth century, those were rare and welcome virtues. Barbarian hoards still threatened the frontier. Norse raiders still terrorized the coastline. And petty feudal rivalries continued to paralyze the interior. After the fall of Rome in 476, Europe had lost its center of gravity and became a spinning dreidel. Though Byzantium continued to flourish in the East, it was not until the slow but steady encroachment of medievalism covered the entire continent that any measure of peace or harmony could be secured. Dympna's character offered tangible hope that the high aspirations of Christian civilization could be—and indeed would be—one day achieved. Thus, her work on behalf of the distressed was widely heralded.

Perhaps too widely.

Eadburh, upon hearing of his daughter's whereabouts, followed her to Gheel. There was an awful confrontation. When she refused to return home with him, he flew into a rage and slew her.

Amazingly, Dympna's vision did not die with her that day. Stricken with sorrow, the citizens of Gheel decided to continue her mission of mercy. Her medieval ethic took root in their lives and became their work. That work continues to the present day: it includes a hospital for the mentally ill, a foundling center, an adoption agency, and the world's largest and most efficient boarding-out program for the afflicted and disturbed—run as a private and decentralized association by the Christian families of Gheel.

The Dark Ages

The medieval period has commonly been called the Dark Ages—as if the light of civilization had been unceremoniously snuffed out. It has similarly been dubbed the Middle Ages—as if it were a gaping parenthesis in mankind's long upward march to modernity.

It was, in fact, anything but dark or middling. Perhaps our greatest fault is that we have limited ourselves by a parochialism in time. It is difficult for us to attribute anything but backwardness to those epochs and cultures that do not share our goals or aspirations.

The medieval period was actually quite remarkable for its many advances, perhaps unparalleled in all of history. It was a true *nascence,* while the epoch that followed was but a *re-naissance.* It was a new and living thing that gave flower to a culture marked by energy and creativity. From the monolithic security of Byzantium in the East to the reckless diversity of feuding fiefs in the West, it was a glorious crazy quilt of human fabrics, textures, and hues.

Now to be sure, the medieval world was racked with abject poverty, ravaging plagues, and petty wars—much like our own day. It was haunted by superstition, prejudice, and corruption—as is the modern era. And it was beset by consuming ambition, perverse sin, and damnable folly—again, so like today. Still, it was free from the kind of crippling sophistication, insular ethnocentricity, and cosmopolitan provincialism that now shackles us, and so it was able to advance astonishingly.

The titanic innovations medievalism brought forth were legion: It gave birth to all the great universities of the world from Oxford and Cambridge to Leipzig and Mainz; it oversaw the establishment of all the great hospitals of the world from St. Bartholomew's and Bedlam in London to St. Bernard's and Voixanne in Switzerland; it brought forth the world's most celebrated artists from Michelangelo Buonarotti and Albrecht Durer to Leonardo da Vinci and Jan van Eyck; it gave us the splendor of Gothic architecture, unmatched and unmatchable to this day, from Notre Dame and Chartres to Winchester and Cologne; it thrust out into howling wilderness and storm-tossed seas the most

accomplished explorers from Amerigo Vespucci and Marco
Polo to Vasco da Gama and Christopher Columbus; it produced some of the greatest minds and most fascinating
lives mankind has yet known (were the list not so sterling it
might begin to be tedious) Copernicus, Dante, Giotto,
Becket, Gutenberg, Chaucer, Charlemagne, Wyclif, Magellan, Botticelli, Donatello, Petrarch, and Aquinas.

But of all the great innovations that medievalism
wrought, the greatest of all was spiritual. Medieval culture—both East and West—was first and foremost Christian
culture. Its life was shaped almost entirely by Christian concerns. Virtually all of its achievements were submitted to
the cause of the gospel. From great cathedrals and gracious
chivalry to long crusades and beautiful cloisters, every manifestation of its presence was somehow tied to its utter and
complete obeisance to Christ's kingdom.

Of course, the medieval church had its share of dangerous and scandalous behavior. It had gross libertines and
rank heretics. It had false professors and bold opportunists.
It had brutal ascetics and imbalanced tyrants. But then,
there was no more of that sort of heterodoxy than we have
today in evangelical, catholic, or orthodox circles—and
perhaps, considering recent headlines, a good deal less.

At any rate, spiritual concerns played a larger role in
the lives of medieval man and women than at almost any
other time before or since. And, as might be expected, that
all-pervading interest was evidenced in a prominent concern for the protection of innocent life.[3] Dympna was by
no means alone in her concern.

Courtly Noblesse

As the medieval Christian culture progressively permeated
the European continent and beyond, mercy and justice for
the weak, the helpless, the infirm, the unborn, and the
poor were given new and vital expression. The tired old
holdovers from paganism—abortion, infanticide, abandon-

ment, and exposure—were gradually and systematically rooted out. Careful provision was made for the victims of lingering lasciviousness. And legal legacies were established to ensure a better and brighter future.

Moving out in concentric circles, the notion that the sanctity of all human life was to be codified—not only in theory, but in practice—dominated legal and ecclesiastical pronouncements. It eventually even found its way into the core of the chivalrous code of courtly noblesse.

As early as the reign of the Byzantine Emperor Justinian in the sixth century, pro-life legislation was universally and comprehensively enforced. Justinian's code was explicit in both prohibiting abortion and exposure and in protecting the victims of harsh circumstance from servile exploitation:

> Those who expose children, possibly hoping they would die, and those who use the potions of the abortionist, are subject to the full penalty of the law—both civil and ecclesiastical—for murder. Should exposure occur, the finder of the child is to see that he is baptized and that he is treated with Christian care and compassion. They may be then adopted as *ad scriptitiorum*—even as we ourselves have been adopted into the kingdom of grace. But, no one may claim as his own—under the rubric of lordship, legal obligation, or servile tenure—an exposed infant. Without distinction, those who are reared in this way by such persons are to be regarded as free and freeborn persons, and they may acquire and dispose of property as they wish, to their own heirs or others, untouched by any taint of servitude or legal subordination or condition of serfdom. This is to be enforced not only by the authorities of the provinces, but also by the bishops, by all officials, by civic leaders and officeholders, and by every government agency.[4]

In the next century, a large ecumenical council met in Vaison to reiterate and expand that pro-life mandate by encouraging the faithful to care for the unwanted and to give relief to the distressed:

> Concerning the care of unwanted and abandoned children spared the murderous designs of the abortionist by legal restraints but still subject more to the wiles of dogs in the street than to the sops of mercy in the home: it has seemed best to make expeditious provision for adoption—even as heaven made for us. Anyone who finds an unwanted child should immediately notify the church from whence the pastor shall announce the same from the altar. If after this very careful disposition, anyone who exposed the child maliciously shall be discovered, he is to be punished with the civil and ecclesiastical sanctions for murder.[5]

About a decade later, another council met at Arles where the Vaison edict was repeated, provision by provision, but with one important addition:

> An heritage is by no means to be scorned or spurned, children being the greatest heritage of all. Therefore, any and all means must be effected to safeguard their well-being—from their quickening in the womb to their assumption of powers.[6]

In the tenth century, a council met at Rouen which not only encouraged Christians to provide positive alternatives to crisis pregnancy situations, but it also enjoined them to guard innocent life with their own lives:

> The eternal rewards to benefactors of the helpless are manifold, but the blood-guiltiness of the stiff-necked will be published abroad. Forbear not to deliver them that are drawn away unto death and them which are ready to be slaughtered.[7]

In the eleventh century, when Burchard of Worms compiled an encyclopedic collection of ecclesiastical canons, he found only consensus and concurrence with Vaison, Arles, and Rouen:

The voice of the church universally announces the holy sanctity of all life. Protection is secured against all aggressors, both within and without the domain of paterfamilias in accordance with the enactments of the most devout, pious, and august princes and lords.[8]

Likewise, a century later when Ivo of Chartes and Gratian compiled more than four thousand previous canons into their respective *Decretums,* affirmation of the culture's longstanding commitment to life was a foregone conclusion:

Fearfully and wonderfully made are all the works of the Almighty. The possessor of all reins, He has covered each soul from the womb. To presume upon that sacred trust is but anathema.[9]

In addition to these juridical pronouncements, a vast treasury of pro-life homiletical material was produced by the most articulate spokesmen of the church throughout the medieval epoch. No doubt those sermons impassioned the minds and informed the hearts of the common people in addition to keeping the issue ever before them. A place on the church's liturgical calendar was even set apart for a pro-life emphasis—the Feast of the Holy Innocents, celebrated on December 28 in the West and December 31 in the East.

Vision and Service

Medieval Christians understood only too well that it was not enough for them to merely affirm the pro-life policies of the state or confess the pro-life dogmas of the church. Like Dympna, they comprehended their responsibility to practically and tangibly act on those policies and dogmas. They knew that just as God had shown them mercy, they were to demonstrate mercy to others (see 2 Corinthians 1:3–7). They knew that just as God had adopted them when they were cast off and rejected, they were to reciprocate (see Deuteronomy 24:17–22).

They realized that this was an essential aspect of true discipleship. After all, Jesus Himself was a servant (see Luke 22:27). He came to serve, not to be served (see Matthew 20:28). He came offering mercy at every turn (see Mark 5:19; Matthew 9:13). And He called His disciples to a similar life of selfless giving (see Luke 22:26). He called them to be servants (see Matthew 19:30). He said, "Whoever wishes to be chief among you, let him be your servant" (Matthew 20:27). He said, "Be merciful, just as your Father is merciful" (Luke 6:36). The attitude of all aspiring leaders was to be "the same as Christ's, who, being in very nature God, did not consider equality with God something to be grasped, but made Himself nothing, taking the very nature of a servant" (Philippians 2:5–7).

And so, faithful followers of Christ in the medieval period founded pro-life mercy ministries throughout Europe and beyond—hospitals, orphanages, almshouses, charitable societies, relief agencies, hostels, and shelters. Monasteries opened their doors to oblate children—the unwanted who were given to the church. Towns and villages kept treasuries of alms, gifts for the needy. The remnants of the old heathenism were driven out of the dark edges of the culture and out of existence. Dympna's heroics were matched by hundreds, perhaps even thousands, of others of equal valor and fruitfulness:

- *Maedoc of Ferns* was an early Irish believer who traveled and studied widely throughout the British Isles in his youth. He established a Christian community in Wexford where he gave shelter to numbers of infant children who survived primitive abortion surgeries at the hands of pagan Druids. Throughout his life, he fought against their deadly rites. He died in 626, but the community has survived to the present day, and it continues to provide institutional care for the helpless and the unwanted.

- *John of Amathus* was born in Cyprus toward the end of the sixth century. The greater part of his life was spent engaged in public service and civil affairs. He married young and faithfully raised his children in the nurture and admonition of the Lord. Despite the fact that he was entirely untrained in theology, his unflagging piety and wisdom encouraged the people of Alexandria to call him at the age of fifty to be their patriarch and pastor. He threw himself into his new responsibilities with characteristic zeal. He injected new life into that old church by establishing innumerable ministries to the needy. He endowed several health care institutions, including the very first maternity hospital. He founded several homes for the aged and infirm. He opened hospices and lodges for travelers. He tore down the remnants of the old infanticide walls outside the city with his own hands and called on his parishioners to join him in defending the sanctity of human life in the future. So prolific were his good deeds that he eventually became known as John the Almsgiver.

- During much of the seventh century, *Adamnan of Iona* was an influential Irish missionary, pastor, author, and civic leader. In 697, he was instrumental in the drafting and enacting of legislation designed to protect women and children from the brutal oppression of the times, including coercive abortion. To this day, this pro-life legal precedent, called *Adamnan's Law*, is the foundation upon which much of Ireland's family policy is built.

- As a young woman, *Bathild of Chelles* was carried away from her English home by pirates and indentured to the court of Clovis II, ruler of the Frankish kingdom. Her great beauty attracted the attentions of the king, and he made her his wife in 651. Some years later, upon the king's death, Bathild became regent for their eldest son, Chlotar III. Utilizing the powers of her office, she stridently opposed the profligate slave trade and the practice of infanticide, exposure, abandonment, and abortion. Her benefactions resulted in a fundamental reorientation of the French legal code that survived virtually unchanged until the Enlightenment a millennium later.

- *Boniface of Crediton* spent the first forty years of his life in quiet service to the church near his home in Exeter. He discipled young converts, cared for the sick, and administered relief for the poor. He was a competent scholar as well, expounding Bible doctrine for a small theological center and compiling the first Latin grammar written in England. But in 718, Boniface left the comfort and security of this life to become a missionary to the savage Teutonic tribes of Germany. For thirty years, he not only proclaimed to them the gospel of light, he portrayed to them the gospel of life. Stories of his courageous intervention on behalf of the innocent abound. He was constantly jeopardizing his own life for the sake of the unborn, the young, the vulnerable, the weak, the helpless, the aged, the sick, and the poor— often throwing his body between the victims and their oppressors. When he was well over seventy, he and his companions were set upon by heathen Frieslanders and put to the sword.

- The legendary generosity and charity of *Wenceslas of Bohemia* is no mere Christmas fable. The young prince lived a life fraught with conflict and tragedy. Both his mother and grandmother—victims of court intrigue and anti-Christian conspiracy—were murdered when he was young. He himself was the object of several assassination attempts and revolts. Yet, despite such adversity, he was a model Christian regent. He outlawed abandonment. He criminalized abortion. He reformed the penal system. And he exercised great compassion on the poor. When he was finally killed by rival heathen elements in the court, he was grievously mourned by his subjects.

- *Margaret of Scotland* was another royal pro-life benefactor. Granddaughter of Edmund Ironside, king of the English, her family sought refuge in Scotland following the Norman conquest in 1066. Four years later, she married Malcolm of Canmore, king of the Scots. They had a wonderful romance and a happy marriage, rearing six sons and two daughters. A strong-willed queen, she was noted for her solicitude for orphans and the poor and for her rabid intolerance of slavery, abandonment, and abortion. Her son David became one of the best Scottish kings, and like his mother came to be revered as a saint for his pro-life concerns and his selfless generosity toward the needy. Her daughter married Henry I of England and brought a similar saintly influence to the British royal line. Thus, by the time she died in 1093, Margaret had not only left her gracious mark on her subjects, she had left it on the whole of the fabric of history.

- *Julian Katarva* was a Dalamatian nobleman who through a tragic error was responsible for the deaths of several members of his family. He never fully recovered from that awful accident and devoted the rest of his life to the care of the sick, the troubled, or the suffering. He endowed several hospitals all over central Europe during the eleventh century. He also went on a personal crusade against those who took life lightly: abortionists, mercenaries, highwaymen, and occultists. Several times he risked his own life by rescuing children or women in distress. Eventually, he became known as Julian the Hospitaller.

- The beautiful and beguiling *Elizabeth of Bratislava* was the daughter of the Hungarian king, Andrew II. Her marriage at the age of fourteen to Ludwig of Thuringia, though arranged for political reasons, was a happy one and the couple had three children. In 1227, Ludwig died suddenly after joining a band of crusaders bound for the Holy Land. Grief stricken for some months, the young Elizabeth finally vowed to give the rest of her life in service to the needy. She helped to establish one of the first foundling hospitals in Europe, as well as several orphanages and almshouses.

- One of the greatest minds of the medieval period was *Bonaventure of Bagnorea*. A brilliant Franciscan theologian and apologist, he was also a devoted philanthropist. Over the long span of his life, he worked in hospitals, orphanages, foundling homes, hospices, monasteries, poor schools, and mendicant clinics. Always a peacemaker, he was a friend to both Thomas Aquinas and the Patriarch of Constantinople—in fact, he was at least partially responsible for the great council at Lyons in 1274 when the Eastern and Western churches were briefly reconciled. Even so, he made no peace nor attempted any reconciliation with the minions of death that did a booming trade in abortifacients, pessaries, and laminaria. His passion to protect the sanctity of human life was incorruptible.

The list of medieval pro-life heroes is very nearly endless: Gregory the Great (d. 604), Cuthbert of Lindisfarne (d. 687), Giles Aegidius (d. 796), Clement Slovensky (d. 916), Edburga of Winchester (d. 960), Dunstan of Canterbury (d. 988), Edward the Confessor (d. 1066), Sava of Trnova (d. 1235), Louis of France (d. 1270), and Elizabeth of Portugal (d. 1336).

By their faith and by their actions, these Christians brought about a revolution in human history. For the first time there was a consensus that life was sacred, that it ought to be protected, and that God would bless any culture that did. By the modern era, that kind of thinking—though once again threatened to one degree or another—had become like the atmosphere: so taken for granted that its marvelously sustained innovation goes fairly unnoticed. But, for the medieval church, such an attitude was of cataclysmic import.

Conclusion

Before the explosive and penetrating growth of medieval Christian influence, the primordial evils of abortion, infanticide, abandonment, and exposure were a normal part of everyday life in Europe. Afterward, they were regarded as the grotesque perversions that they actually are. That remarkable new pro-life consensus was detonated by a cultural reformation of cosmic proportions. It was catalyzed by civil decrees, ecclesiastical canons, and merciful activity. And it revolved around five fundamental principles:

Orthodoxy

The movement to preserve, protect, and nurture life during the medieval era was purposefully grounded in the orthodox truths of Scripture. As Christocentric cultures, both the East in Byzantium and the West in Europe strove to live out their concerns in the world according to the dictates of the sovereign Creator. Believers were driven to conform all matters of faith and practice to the covenantal comprehension that God is both transcendent and immanent—and that He is to be honored in all circumstances and situations.

The Church

The medieval pro-life movement was first and foremost an outgrowth of the ministry of the church. It was a societal manifestation of God's work of covenantal reconciliation, beginning in the church and moving outward in concentric circles. Every effort on behalf of innocent life—from the criminalization of abandonment to the care of the unwanted—had its genesis in the sacramental Body of Christ. The medieval church—despite all our preconceived notions about its monolithic uniformity—was remarkably diverse. Yet in the substantive areas of the gospel, it maintained steadfast unity; and because the pro-life movement was essentially a movement of the church, it too was marked by an unwavering solidarity.

Servanthood

Ethical service was a hallmark of the medieval pro-life movement. In every way, the believers sought to earn the right to speak authoritatively into the lives of the hurting and the desperate through selfless deeds of charity. In this way, the pro-life heroes saturated the culture with a clear-cut word-*and*-deed message of grace, mercy, and truth.

Urgency

In order to preserve the sanctity of life, medieval pro-life heroes had to sacrifice sorely. In the face of God's judgment, they gave of themselves—of their time, their energy, their money, and their resources. All too often, they were forced to lay their reputations on the line and sometimes even their lives. Despite danger, hardship, and suffering, they held their ground against the onslaught of abortion, infanticide, abandonment, and exposure because of the high and urgent call of the gospel.

Patience

The multi-generational perspective of the medieval Christians enabled them to place their passion and urgency in perspective. It enabled them to work over the long haul. It enabled them to plan, build, and project. It enabled them to gradually and systematically establish a heritage that could be passed from father to son to grandson to great-grandson.

ɚ   ɚ   ɚ

Assaults on the bastion of that great medieval legacy have been fierce and furious during the five-hundred-odd years since the fall of Constantinople and the passing of the medieval mantle. But battered and bedraggled as it is, it still stands—vivid testimony to the depth of its foundation.

PART 2

THE
SECOND TIME
AROUND

To comprehend the history of a thing is to unlock the mysteries of its present, and more, to disclose the profundities of its future.
Hilaire Belloc

All that was good in Feudalism is gone: the good humor, the common sports, the apportioned duties, the fraternity that could live without equality. All that is bad in Feudalism not only remains but grows: the caprice, the sudden cruelty, the offence to human dignity in the existence of slave and lord.
G. K. Chesterton

4

CASTLES IN THE AIR: THE RENAISSANCE AND THE ENLIGHTENMENT

per angusta ad augusta [1]

> There is a complex knot of forces underlying any nation once Christian; a smoldering of the old fires.
>
> Hilaire Belloc

> Intent on its ending, they are ignorant of its beginning; and therefore of its very being.
>
> G. K. Chesterton

he remarkable explosion of wealth, knowledge, and technology that occurred during the Renaissance and the Enlightenment completely reshaped human society. No institution was left untouched.

Families were transformed from mere digits within the larger baronial or communal clan into nuclear societies in and of themselves. Local communities were shaken from their sleepy timidity and thrust into the hustle bustle of mercantilism and urbanization. The church was rocked by the convulsions of the Reformation, the Counter-Reformation, anabaptism, deism, and neo-paganism. Kingdoms, fiefs, baronies, and principalities began to take the torturous path toward becoming modern nation states.

Such revolutionary changes are not without cost. Ultimately, the cost to Christian civilization—both East and West—was devastating. Immorality and corruption ran rampant. Disparity between rich and poor became endemic. Ruthless and petty wars multiplied beyond number. Even the old horrors of abortion, infanticide, abandonment, and exposure began to recur in the urban and industrialized centers.

Vincent De Paul was born for such a time as this—to tackle such problems as these.

Raised the son of a peasant farmer in Gascony, he surrendered to the ministry at the age of twenty. Spurred on by a passionate concern for the poor and neglected, he quickly developed a thriving outreach to the decayed gentry, deprived peasantry, galley-slaves, unwanted children, and convicts of France. Over the ensuing years, he mobilized hundreds of Christians for charitable work and established innumerable institutions—hospitals, shelters, foundling centers, orphanages, and almshouses throughout all of Europe.

In 1652, Vincent was horrified to discover that a guild of midwives had begun performing illicit abortions in the slums of Paris. He quickly went to work, organizing relief and proper medical supervision for the children that had somehow survived the procedures, as well as the women that had been injured by them. He lobbied the magistrates to effect appropriate civil justice. He prodded the church to exercise spiritual discipline. And he appealed to merchants and businessmen to lift up their voices of concern and to exercise their prerogatives of privilege.

He also launched a complete investigation of the grisly trade, drawing public attention to the issue and provoking public ire against the whole sordid affair. At one point, he actually went undercover to infiltrate the covert meetings of the guild. He gathered crucial information from the inside that enabled him to more effectively do battle with the myrmidons of death.

Despite the fact that the free spirit of the Renaissance and the Enlightenment had swept across the culture like a prairie fire, Vincent's efforts struck a responsive note among a faithful remnant. They rejected the siren's song of the day and embraced the values and virtues of life. They developed a comprehensive plan of service to the victims of the crime and a concerted program of opposition to the perpetrators of the crime.

Vincent made it clear to his fellow-laborers that such activity was not an option for the believer—it was mandatory. He said:

> When'ere God's people gather, there is life in the midst of them—yea, Christ's gift to us as a people is life, and that more abundantly. To protect the least of these, our brethren, with everything that God has placed at our disposal is not merely facultative, it is exigent. In addition though, it is among the greatest and most satisfying of our sundry stewardships.[2]

By the time he died in 1660, the pro-life movement he had sparked was alive and well—alert to the threat against the innocents that inevitably comes when men turn their hearts away from Christ and toward the delusions of this world (see Proverbs 8:32). To this day all around the globe, members of the Society of Vincent De Paul continue the momentum that he began by modeling a life of obedience to the high call of the gospel.

The Renaissance Relapse

Despite its many advances in art, music, medicine, science, and technology, the Renaissance and Enlightenment were essentially nostalgic revivals of ancient pagan ideals and values. The dominating ideas of the times were classical humanism, pregnable naturalism, and antinomian individualism—or in other words: godlessness, materialism, and hedonism. Taking their cues primarily from ancient Greece and Rome, the leaders of the epoch were not so much interested in the Christian notion of *progress* as they were in the heathen ideal of *innocence*. Reacting to the artificialities and contrivances of the medieval period, they dispatched the Christian consensus it had wrought with enervating aplomb. In short, they threw the baby out with the bath.

Throughout history men have reacted instead of acted in times of crisis. They have sought to ameliorate an ill on the right hand by turning immediately and entirely to the left. They have tried to solve a problem in the citadels of the present by desecrating the foundations of the past. Driven by extremism, they have failed to see the moderating application of adjustments and alternatives.

We fall into that same trap today. Instead of attempting to reform, refurbish, or renovate, we want to rip asunder the roots of the ages and start over from scratch. The result of such ludicrous impudence is invariably disastrous. When faced with economic inequity and injustice, our first reaction is to bureaucratically centralize the means of production and distribution—instead of actually creating new opportunities and incentives for the poor. When faced with the problem of hunger in the Third World, our inclination is to sterilize mothers, denude traditional authority, and collectivize property—instead of actually promoting development projects that can help transform poverty into productivity. When faced with the rising tide of promiscuity, sexually transmitted diseases, and undesired pregnancies, our initial response is to defile the minds of our youngsters, kill off our progeny, and equip our teens with powerful recreational drugs—instead of actually inculcating the values of moral purity, responsibility, and integrity.

When faced with the recalcitrance of feudal life, the immediate reaction of the people of the Renaissance and Enlightenment was to reject out of hand the very foundations of their Christian heritage—instead of actually building on that heritage for the future. Nothing was sacred any longer. Everything—every thought, word, and deed; every hope, dream, and aspiration; every tradition, institution, and relationship—was redefined.

No society can long stand without some ruling set of principles, some overriding values, or some ethical standard. Thus, when the men and women of the sixteenth through the eighteenth centuries threw off Christian mores, they necessarily went casting about for a suitable alternative. And so, Greek and Roman thought was exhumed from the ancient sarcophagus of paganism. Aristotle, Plato, and Pythagoras were dusted off, dressed up, and rehabilitated as the newly tenured voices of wisdom. Cicero, Seneca, and Herodotus were raised from the philosophical crypt and made to march to the tune of a new era.

Every forum, every arena, and every aspect of life began to reflect this newfound fascination with the pre-Christian past. Art, architecture, music, drama, literature, and every other form of popular culture began to portray the themes of classical humanism, pregnable naturalism, and antinomian individualism.

And they began to extol their pre-Christian values as well, including the values of abortion, infanticide, abandonment, and exposure. A complete reversion took place. Virtually all the great advances that the medieval era brought were lost in just a few short decades.

By the middle of the epoch, as many as one out of every three children was killed or exposed in French, Italian, and Spanish cities. In Toulouse, the rate of known abandonment as a percentage of the number of recorded births varied from an approximate mean of 10 percent at the beginning of the era to a mean of about 17 percent at its end—with the final decades consistently above 20 and often passing 25 percent for the whole population of the city. In the poorer quarters of the city, the rate may have reached as high as 40 percent. In Lyons before the French Revolution, the number of cast-off, unwanted infants was approximately one-third the number of births. During the same period in Paris, children known to have been abandoned accounted for between 20 and 30 percent of all registered births. In Florence the rate ranged from a low of 14 percent of all babies to a high of just under 45 percent. In Milan, the opening of the age witnessed a rate of 16 percent. By its closing the percentage had actually risen to about 25 percent. In Madrid, the figures ranged anywhere from 14 to 26 percent, while in London, they were between 11 and 22 percent. Fragmentary evidence suggests comparable rates throughout the rest of Europe, wherever resurrected paganism was extolled.

Once again, the horrid barbarity of promiscuous child-killing became a matter of course in this poor fallen world. In some circles it even became a badge of some honor: Jean-Jacques Rousseau, for example, boasted that he had abandoned all five of his illegitimate children while Mozart, Fielding, Goethe, Chatterton, Diderot, Swift, Goya, Voltaire, and Defoe all explored the idea in their works.

Clearly, the minions of death were back. And they were back with a vengeance.

Although a number of communities tried to maintain a legislative hedge of protection around the innocents, the wholesale infiltration of pagan concepts into the culture—and even into the church—made it practically impossible. The rising tide was just too much.

The Reformation and Counter-Reformation

Throughout the entire fifteenth century, cries for the reformation of the church came from every sector. The church had become impotent; it was entirely unable to halt the rapid slide into the godlessness, materialism, and hedonism of the ancient pagan philosophies. Slowly but surely, the church had lost its grip.

In the East, the fall of Constantinople and the subsequent captivity of much of Orthodoxy had made that once formidable force in Christendom of little influence. While in the West, rampant simony, monastic corruption, inquisitional fury, and infighting between orders had stymied the effectiveness of Catholicism. Meanwhile, popular culture took its nasty turn away from truth.

So, from traditionalists to innovators, from mendicants to oblates, from magistrates to hierarchs, and from those who had vested interests to those entirely on the outside of the system—everyone agreed that the church had to somehow find its way. It was evident to even the most disinterested observer that the church must revitalize if it were to continue to give direction, vision, and purpose to the culture.

No one disagreed on the fact *that* the church needed to be reformed. What they disagreed on was *what* that reform should entail and *how* it was to be effected. In frustrated tension, dozens of competing factions, sects, schisms, rifts, and divisions roiled just beneath the surface of the church's tranquility for decades. Finally, on October 31, 1517, those pent-up passions burst out into the open when an Augustinian monk named Martin Luther posted his ninety-five theses on the door of the Palast Church in Wittenberg. In a single stroke, not one, but two momentous renewal movements were launched that at last were able to effect genuine reform within the church: the Protestant Reformation and the Catholic Counter-Reformation.

Ostensibly opposed to one another, these two movements actually worked in tandem to transform and even revive the church. The intensity of the Biblical and ecclesiastical controversy they provoked brought a new level of commitment and integrity to both sides of the conflict—so that even though the tragic breach of catholicity had become apparently irreparable, the ability of Christians to deal with the insidious cultural problems actually improved. Legions of faithful believers on both sides of the rift began to exercise renewed spiritual fervor. Protestants and Catholics alike began anew to take their responsibilities seriously. They began to stand firm in the face of encroaching heathenism. And they began to enter into the battle for life.

The elimination altogether of the monasteries and religious orders of northern Europe following the meliorations of the Reformers necessitated a whole new approach to pro-life activity there. Similarly, the house-cleaning of the Counter-Reformation produced new conditions in southern Europe that made many of the old medieval pro-life methodologies and institutions obsolescent. But rather than being an obstacle to the ministry of mercy and compassion, these new situations and circumstances actually became a catalyst for growth and maturity.

And once again, the church was unanimous in its commitment to life. John Calvin, the leader of the Swiss Reformation said:

> The unborn child . . . though enclosed in the womb of its mother, is already a human being . . . and should not be robbed of the life which it has not yet begun to enjoy. If it seems more horrible to kill a man in his own house than in a field, because a man's house is his place of most secure refuge, it ought surely to be deemed more atrocious to destroy an unborn child in the womb before it has come to light.[3]

Defense of the innocents, he argued, was so integral and indistinguishable from a defense of the gospel that believers ought to be just as willing to risk severe persecution for the one as for the other:

> Now to suffer persecution for righteousness' sake is a singular comfort. For it ought to occur to us how much honor God bestows upon us in thus furnishing us with the special badge of His soldiery. I say that not only they that labor for the defense of the gospel, but they that in any way maintain the cause of righteousness suffer persecution for righteousness. Therefore, whether declaring God's truth against Satan's falsehoods or in taking up

the protection of the good and innocent against the wrongs of the wicked, we must undergo the offenses and hatred of the world, which may imperil either our life, our fortunes, or our honor.[4]

Similarly, Ignatius Loyola, one of the most prominent figures of the Counter-Reformation, asserted:

Life is God's most precious gift. To scorn it by any sort of murderous act—such as the abortion of a child—is not merely an awful tyranny, it is a smear against the integrity of God as well. Suffer as we must, even die if need be, such rebellion against heaven must not be free to run its terrible courses.[5]

In edict after edict, council after council, canon after canon, and synod after synod, the church never once wavered—affirming its historical and Biblical commitment to uphold, rescue, and defend innocent life at all costs.

Action and Truth

Christians during this epoch understood only too well the Biblical mandate to "not merely love in word and tongue but in action and truth" (1 John 3:18). Thus, the church's unanimity on the sanctity of human life was not merely rhetorical; it was translated into action. Homes for girls in crisis were established, maternity and foundling hospitals were endowed, lobbying efforts were begun, legislation was enacted, research was funded, and direct action rescues were launched. The stories of individual and corporate heroism are both multitudinous and manifold:

- *Thomas of Villanueva* grew up in the region of Don Quixote's La Mancha in a devout Christian home where virtuous living and gracious charity were constantly modeled for him by his parents. It was no surprise then when he committed himself to a life of Christian service after graduating from the new university at Alcala. In 1518, at the age of thirty, he was ordained and began a brilliant career as an anointed and effective preacher. His ministry was most distinguished not only by his very evident pulpit skills however, but rather by his care and concern for the poor and needy. He was especially involved in providing relief for abused children and orphans—securing new homes for them as well as meeting their immediate material needs. He was involved in other pro-life activities as well: once, when he discovered an abortion cabal operating illicitly in a nearby city, he flew into a frenzy of righteous indignation, provoking a criminal investigation and eliciting stronger laws for the protection of children.

- A devoted son of the Scottish Reformation, *Andrew Geddes* was involved in a ministry to abandoned and orphaned children throughout all the fierce religious conflicts that racked his tiny nation in the sixteenth century. Converted under the preaching of John Knox, he served as a deacon in that great Reformer's church. Taking his cue from the apostolic injunctions in the Bible, he utilized that office as a channel of mercy to the needy. In addition, a translation of Jean Luis Vives' widely read treatise, *On the Help of the Poor,* left a deep impression on Geddes—so much so in fact, that he used the book as a model for his various pro-life activities. A Scottish Presbyterian utilizing the work of a Spanish Catholic as a guide to ministry in the church of John Knox may seem rather incongruous from this juncture in history, but for Geddes, the mandate to care for the innocent superceded jurisdictional or denominational obstacles—and the result was that the work of the ministry proceeded apace.

- A sudden and glorious conversion transformed *Camillus de Lellis* from a gruff soldier of fortune into a meek and compassionate servant of Christ. Because he himself had suffered from a chronic affliction, shortly after his decision to trust the Lord, he offered himself to the hospital of San Giacomo in Rome, of which he quickly became bursar. This experience opened his eyes to the shocking brutalities of Renaissance life. He began to train and supervise teams of Christian workers not only to care for the sick but also to deal with some of the entrenched problems of the poor, the homeless, and the abandoned that led to disease and contagion. Before the end of the sixteenth century, he had established several hospitals and hospices in Naples to handle the second- and third-order consequences of child-killing and other neo-pagan practices.

- In 1625, *Nicholas Ferrar* retired from a parliamentary career in London and moved with the families of his brother and brother-in-law to a small Christian community in Huntingdonshire. The community was marked by extreme Puritan piety: twice a day they all attended the liturgical offices in their tiny church, and at every hour during the day some members joined in a little office of prayer, so that the whole Psalter was recited daily; and at night, at least two members of the household were watching and the Psalter was again recited. They were also marked by their charity and pro-life activism as well. Ferrar focused their concern on abandoned boys that roamed the byways. Though he died in 1637, the community developed one of the most effective Christian alternatives to the humanism of the day through simple Christian service and unfaltering spiritual devotion.

- *Louise De Marillac* married a high official of the French court and enjoyed a life of privilege and pleasure. Her husband's death left her a widow at the age of thirty-three. That tragedy effected in her a deep desire to serve Christ, and she committed herself to His kingdom. Shortly thereafter, she became a companion and co-worker of Vincent De Paul in Paris, caring for the sick and helpless. With him, she launched a sheltering ministry for women in crisis. At the time of her death, the ministry had more than forty houses throughout France and twenty-six more in Paris where women could come and escape the pressures of abortion advocates, and where they could learn to rebuild their lives.

- *Otto Blumhardt* was one of the earliest Lutheran missionaries to Africa. Setting out alone in the first decade of
  the seventeenth century at a time when most of that
  great continent still remained unexplored and uncharted, he took the message of Christ and His glorious grace to several primitive jungle tribes—learning
  their languages, caring for their sick, and training their
  young. When he encountered gruesome child-killing
  rites in several of the tribes, he was not startled in the
  least—witnessing abortion and exposure during his
  childhood in the slums of Hildeshelm had prepared
  him for the depths of depravity in fallen man. That is
  not to say that he accepted it as a matter of course. On
  the contrary, for the rest of his life, he devoted himself
  to the fight for human life. By the time of his death in
  1632, he was known by the natives of the region as the
  "Father of the Jungle" because so many of them literally owed their lives—their very existence—to his faithfulness.

- *John Eudes* was born in Normandy at a time when anti-
  clerical and anti-Christian sentiment was at a fever
  pitch. Because his parents remained pious, he tasted
  the bitter draught of discrimination early in life. Not
  surprisingly, as an adult he dedicated himself to the
  care of the persecuted—refugees, the feebleminded,
  Jews, the sick, Huguenots, and mendicants. He even organized teams of Christian women to care for women
  reclaimed from prostitution. His fearless and selfless
  care of the dying distinguished him during two virulent
  epidemics that swept through France in 1634 and 1639.
  But his greatest work involved his crusade against child-
  killing. Like so many faithful Christians before him, he
  took seriously and literally the injunction to "rescue
  those being dragged away to the slaughter" (Proverbs
  24:11). Innumerable times he stopped abortionists
  from plying their black arts by placing his own body
  between the intended victim and its executioner. He
  died at the age of seventy-nine content that he and his

followers had rebuffed the Renaissance of barbarism at least to some degree.

- Education was the privilege of the very few and the very rich until *Jean Baptist De La Salle* began his great work midway through the seventeenth century. After giving up a life of ease, he dedicated himself to teaching the children of the very poor. He opened day schools, Sunday schools, vocational training schools, teachers' colleges, and continuing education centers—actually pioneering many modern techniques and concepts—in more than fourteen cities throughout Europe. He fought hard against the insipid humanistic tendencies within the scholastic community, and he deplored the corresponding decline in Christian morality. He believed that if youngsters could be educated in accordance with gospel principles, the barbarities of abortion and abandonment would disappear; but if they were not given the opportunity to advance, such wickedness would eventually prevail—because, as he often quipped, evil desires nothing better than hopelessness and ignorance.

- *Francis Di Girolamo* was consecrated to the work of the gospel as a very young man. The victim of a very cruel and harsh childhood himself, he pledged his life to the alleviation of the pains and woes of the poor and destitute. In search of sinners, he penetrated into the prisons, the brothels, the galleys, the back lanes, and the tenements of urban Naples. He rescued hundreds of children from deplorable conditions and crusaded against a contraband abortifacient trade that was enjoying a new resurgence. Once he burst into a laboratory where parricides were being concocted and, like Jesus in the Temple, literally decimated the room, overturning the equipment and scattering the drugs single-handedly. Over the years, he opened a thrift shop for the poor, several almshouses, and a foundling hospital. At his funeral in 1716, the poor from miles around thronged the church in grief.

- It was while serving as a surgeon on the British warship *Arundel* that *James Ramsay* got his first glimpse of the conditions of chattel slavery. It would haunt him for the rest of his life and would, in fact, completely redirect his ambitions and abilities. In time, he would submit to a call to the ministry and a mission to free England from the curse of inhuman servitude.[6] A small book of memoirs advocating abolition, which he composed while serving in a quiet village pastorate, placed him at the center of a storm of controversy. Working with some of the greatest Christian thinkers and activists of the day—Granville Sharp, Charles Middleton, Thomas Clarkson, Ignatius Latrobe, and the young William Wilberforce—he applied the principles of the Christian pro-life legacy to the question of slavery. By the time he died in 1789, the erosion of morality that Renaissance and Enlightenment thinking had begun in England had been checked to some degree—and the end of chattel slavery was within sight.

Though certainly the pro-life movement was less prominent than it had been in earlier generations, hundreds of faithful Christians—both Reformed and Catholic—demonstrated beyond any shadow of a doubt that the gospel compels believers to defend life to the uttermost: Angelica of Bresica (d. 1540), Cajetan Gaetano (d. 1547), Charles Borromeo (d. 1584), Benedict the Black (d. 1589), Joseph Calasanz (d. 1648), Jean Bolsec (d. 1657), Martin Laedenton (d. 1694), Edward Ridley (d. 1699), Malcolm Lidds (d. 1771), and Georges Fleures (d. 1788).

Most of these heroes of the faith hardly yearned for the old days of medievalism, and yet they unquestionably drew on its great pro-life legacy. They countered the insipid humanism of their times with reform within and diligence without.

Conclusion

The battle had to be waged all over again. Despite the great gains won for the cause of life throughout the millennium of medievalism, fallen cultures—like fallen men—descend the downgrade whenever the basic principles of the Christian life as revealed in the Scriptures are neglected, ignored, or usurped.

Such was the case with the Renaissance and the Enlightenment. Because that era was marked by a new appreciation for the philosophies of pagan antiquity, the culture soon reverted to the morals of pagan antiquity, including the desecration of life.

Once again, however, Christians responded to the urgent need to protect life. They mobilized efforts on behalf of women in crisis situations, they protected the innocent, and they centered their work in the redemption of Christ. In short, as they revived and renewed the church, they revived and renewed the pro-life movement as well—a movement as old as the gospel itself, but as fresh and new as the dew of the dawn. As before, this revival was rooted in five basic principles:

Orthodoxy

The church was only effective in its task of protecting innocent life when it remained steadfast in doctrinal purity and Scriptural fidelity. Whenever it began to slide into the comfortable heresies of the day, it became compromised and impotent. But whenever it would "earnestly contend for the faith once and for all delivered to the saints" (Jude 3), God blessed its efforts gloriously. Whenever and wherever it took its every cue from the dictates of the sovereign God, it was remarkably successful.

The Church

As the old pagan practices began to creep back into societies during the Renaissance and the Enlightenment, only the sacramental church was able to withstand their subtle profanities. Only the church, with its ingenious balance between hierarchy and egality, was able to manifest an authentic pro-life ethic. As at no other time, the unity of the bride of Christ was shattered during this momentous epoch. The Reformation and the Counter-Reformation unleashed one cataclysm after another on the church. Even so, every authentically Biblical branch of the body[7] remained unanimously committed to the sanctity of life—and they remained committed to a single-minded protection of life. And so as before, only the church was able to offer hope to the hopeless and help to the helpless.

Servanthood

As in the medieval epoch, Christians did not merely oppose child-killing procedures, they worked hard to provide compassionate and effective alternatives for women and children in crisis. They *lived* their message; they didn't just *preach* it. They understood only too well that Christianity is covenantal, and thus it is ethical.

Urgency

It has never been easy defending the defenseless. The costs have always been high. But when lives are at stake, Christians have always been willing to face the odds, even when they themselves were placed in terrible jeopardy. When the judgment of God is nigh, they have always been at the forefront of the struggle for life—even when they themselves had to risk everything that they had and everything that they were.

Patience

It was a life-and-death urgency that motivated the pro-life heroes of the Reformation and the Counter-Reformation to risk all for the unborn, the abused, the abandoned, and the neglected. But it was a sane and solid patience—standing foursquare on the promises of God—that enabled them to sustain their efforts from one generation to the next. And ultimately, it was the wedding of the former with the latter that brought them their consummate success.

         ào   ào   ào

The great pro-life legacy forged by the earliest Christians during the patristic and medieval eras not only survived during the Renaissance and the Enlightenment, but it also thrived. The result was that lives were saved, women were protected, and children were nurtured. In addition, the culture continued to bathe in the good providence of Almighty God.

TO THE UTTERMOST: THE GREAT MISSIONS MOVEMENT

in hoc signo vinces [1]

It is a good thing to have loved one woman from a child, and it is a good thing not to have to return to the faith.

Hilaire Belloc

If a thing is worth doing, it is worth doing badly.

G. K. Chesterton

ndia in the nineteenth century was no place for a lady—or at least, it was no place for an impressionable young lady, born and bred in the comfort and ease of Victorian England. It was a rough and tumble world of stark brutality and crass occultism. It was a chaotic and untamed spiritual desert.

The bestial cult of Kali enslaved millions in wretched fear and perversity. The cruel and impersonal rigors of Brahmanism racked millions more with the fickle whims of fashion and fancy. Still more were gripped in the bizarre downward spiral of fatalistic self-abasement, inhuman social stratification, and raw moral corruption of Vedacism. And besides these divergent branches of Hinduism, a jangling kaleidoscope of competing cosmic visions—Moslem, Sikh, and Buddhist—imposed on the great Asian subcontinent a nasty paganism of anarchy and unrest.

Anna Bowden was a consummate Victorian debutante. She was a lady. But she burst fearlessly onto that awful cultural landscape with faith, hope, and love.

With a remarkable singleness of heart and soul, Anna left her family's comfortable Notting Hill social orbit of staid and privatized Anglicanism to enroll in Henrietta Soltau's mission training school in London. Formed as an adjunct to the work of J. Hudson Taylor's China Inland Mission, the school provided candidate screening and intensive preparation for women who had yielded to the call of overseas evangelization.

Late in 1891, Robert Campbell-Green, an itinerant evangelist working in southern India, visited the school to deliver a short series of devotional talks on the many new missionary inroads that he had recently witnessed in the Mysore, Madras, and Pradesh provinces. He related the brutal realities of the dominant Hindu culture—the awful disrespect of the poor, the weak, the helpless, and the low-born as well as the spiritual captivity to dark and damning passions. Anna was completely mesmerized. She felt an irresistible call to take the good news of the gospel and the succor of Christ to that desperate land. Though only midway through her training, she immediately—almost impulsively—committed herself to the fledgling work there. A month later, she set sail for Conjeeveram.

Her idealistic travel journal conveys the overriding vision that she carried into the work:

> I know not the challenges that face me among peoples who live but for death. I do know, though, the grace of the Savior that has called me to die but for life.[2]

When she arrived in Conjeeveram—a seacoast town about twenty-five miles north of Kancheepuram and about forty miles south of Madras—she discovered that the mission compound of Campbell-Green had been abandoned.

Apparently, there was nothing to indicate what had happened or where the missionaries had gone. The only other English residents in the region, a small community of fabric exporters, could only say that the mission had been vacant for quite some time and that the residents of the compound had suddenly disappeared without a trace.

Despite this staggering turn of events, Anna remained undeterred. Working with the occasional and begrudging aid of the English merchants, she refurbished the mission's decrepit facilities and reopened its tiny clinic and school.

Although most of the local residents generally maintained a cool distance, Anna's tender and magnetic personality drew innumerable children and outcaste "untouchables" into her circle. After only three months, her solitary efforts had begun to reap a bountiful harvest.

It was not long, however, before Anna's jubilant optimism ran headlong into trouble. A fairly new Hindu reform movement, the *Arya Samaj,* had begun to spread in southern India. Dedicated to the purification of Hinduism and a return to the traditional values of ancient paganism, the adherents of *Arya Samaj* were bitterly anti-Western and anti-Christian. They sought a ban on "proselytism" and re-instituted such practices as *immolation* and *sarti*—the ritual sacrifice of widows on the funeral biers of their husbands—as well as *deyana*—female infanticide—and *kananda*—cultic abortifacient procedures. Although a number of very prominent missionaries attempted to adhere to the longstanding British colonial policy of non-interference—including William Miller, the renowned principal of the nearby Christian College of Madras—Anna simply could not stand idly by while the innocents were slaughtered. She immediately set up a rescue network, providing ready escape for damned widows. And she pulled together a cadre of pro-life believers to interfere with the practices and procedures of the abortion guilds.

Describing her motivation for such drastic and dramatic activities, she wrote:

The mandate of Holy Writ is plain. We must clothe the naked, feed the hungry, shelter the shelterless, succor the infirmed, and rescue the perishing. I can do no less and still be faithful to the high call of our Sovereign Lord.[3]

Apparently, her crusade began to exact a toll on the traditionalist Hindu movement because early in 1893, Swami Dayanand Sarasvati, the leader of *Arya Samaj*, appealed to Queen Victoria's viceroy to have Anna stopped. In an attempt to keep the peace, the British administrator ordered Anna to refrain from any activities that were not "directly related to the operation of the missionary outpost."[4] Anna replied saying that rescuing innocent human life was indeed "directly related" to her mission work and that, in fact, it was "directly related to any form of Christian endeavor, humanitarian or evangelistic."

Impatient and dissatisfied with the viceroy's meek handling of Anna, Sarasvati dispatched an angry mob of his followers to the mission compound. They burned several of the buildings to the ground, raped a number of the young girls who had come to live there, and tortured and killed Anna.

But that was not the end of Anna's impact. The "clash of absolutes"[5] that she provoked highlighted for all the world to see the unbridgeable gulf between Christian ethics and heathen brutality.[6] Her daring example sparked a revival within the missionary community in India and her journals, published shortly after her martyrdom, made a stunning impact throughout England. Perhaps most importantly of all, her commitment stimulated and mobilized the church to call on the government to fundamentally alter the essence of the policy of non-interference—not just in India, but wherever the gospel went out around the globe—and to enforce a universal legal code rooted in the Christian notion of the sanctity of life.

Anna Bowden was a lady, an "elect lady" (2 John 1). And, India in the nineteenth century was *just* the place for her.

Colonizing the Globe

The accession of the Christian culture of Europe as the world's dominating sociopolitical force was actually not assured until well into the nineteenth century. In fact, for the bulk of its first two millennia, Christian culture had been strikingly unsuccessful in spreading its deleterious effects beyond European shores. In the Far East, for instance, missionary endeavors were practically non-existent in China and paralyzed by persecution in Japan. In India, the higher castes were virtually untouched by the gospel, and even the lower castes showed only transitory interest. The Islamic lands were as resistant as always to the inroads of the church. South America's conversion to the conquistadors' Catholicism was tenuous at best. And tropical Africa had proven to be so formidable and inhospitable that Western settlements were confined to a few small outposts along the coast. Clearly, Christianity was still very much a white man's religion.

There had been, of course, a few bursts of expansion. In 1453, a series of catastrophic events—both good and bad—freed European monarchs to cast their vision outward for the first time since the early crusades. That year saw the defeat of Constantine XI by Sultan Mohammed II—thus, at long last, bringing to an end the storied Byzantine Empire. In addition, the Hundred Years War between England and France ended, as did the wars between Venice and Milan, Russia and Lithuania, and Prussia and Poland. The Habsburgs and the Medicis were both bolstered in their respective realms. And Guttenberg's press in Mainz altered the transmission of knowledge and culture forever with the publication of the first *printed* book, a Bible.

Explorers began to venture out into uncharted realms. Scientists began to probe long hidden mysteries. Traders and merchants carved out new routes, new markets, and new technologies. Energies that had previously been devoted exclusively to survival were redirected by local magistrates into projects and programs designed to improve health, hygiene, and the common good. Africa, India, China, Indonesia, and the Americas were opened to exploration and exploitation. From colonial outposts there, a tremendous wealth of exotic raw resources poured into European cities.

But despite all these advantages, European advances were limited and short lived, and the gospel made only halting and sporadic progress. Internecine warfare and petty territorialism disrupted—and very nearly nullified— even that much Christian influence. From 1688, when William and Mary concluded the Glorious Revolution in England by ascending to the throne, Louis XIV canonized the iron-fisted notion of "Divine Right," and young Peter Romanov became Czar of all the Russias—until 1848—when the calamitous Marxist rebellions in Paris, Rome, Venice, Berlin, Parma, Vienna, and Milan were finally squelched— Europe was racked by one convulsive struggle after another. During those two centuries, the cause of Christian unity, veracity, and temerity wore a Khazar face—buffeted by the Austro-Prussian Wars, the Napoleonic Wars, the American War of Independence, the Persian-Ottoman Wars, the Sino-Russian Wars, the French Revolution, the Greek and the South American Wars of Independence, and the Mogul Invasions. The entire culture seemed to be driven by an Arimathean impulse to bury disparaged truth.

At last though, a hush of peace fell upon the continent during the Victorian Age: *Pax Britannia.* And within the span of a generation, the message of Christ and the benefits of a Christian culture and law code were impressed upon the whole earth.

Three great revolutions—beginning first in England and then spreading throughout all the European dominions—laid the foundations for this remarkable turn of events. The first was the Agricultural Revolution. The replacement of fallowing with leguminous rotation, the use of chemical fertilizers, and the introduction of farm machinery, enabled Europeans to virtually break the cycle of famine and triage across the continent for the first time in mankind's history. The second was the Industrial Revolution. Manufactured goods and the division of labor created a broad-based middle class and freed the unlanded masses—again, for the first time in human history. The third was the Transportation Revolution. At the beginning of the nineteenth century, Napoleon could not cross his domain any more efficiently than Nebuchadnezzar could have six centuries before Christ. By the end of the Victorian Age, men were racing across the rails and roads in motorized vehicles of stupendous power, they were crashing over and under the waves of the sea in iron vessels of enormous size, and they were cutting through the clouds in ingenious zeppelins, balloons, and planes.

Suddenly, the earth became a European planet. Whole continents were carved up between the rival monarchs. With a thrashing overheated quality—in which charity and good sense were sometimes sacrificed for the practical end of beating the Hun—Africa, Asia, Australia, the Far East, Latin America, and the Middle East became the backyard playgrounds of speculative colonists and imperial opportunists.

The Great Commission

Not long after his heroic journey in 1492, Christopher Columbus confessed that commercial, imperial, or colonial interests were of only minor concern to him. He boldly challenged the common wisdom, confidently plied the sponsorship of the regents of the Spanish kingdom, and fearlessly sailed across the seas. But he did not muster that kind of courage because of Ferdinand and Isabella's aspirations of wealth or their royal commission. Instead, he was inspired and driven by altogether different aspirations and another—still higher—royal commission:

It was the Lord who put it in me to sail from here to the Indies. The fact that the gospel must be preached to so many lands—that is what convinced me. . . . Charting the seas is but a necessary requisite for the fulfillment of the Great Commission of our glorious Savior.[7]

The last mandate of Christ to His disciples, commonly known as the Great Commission, was to comprehensively evangelize all the world. He said:

"All authority in heaven and on earth has been given to me. Therefore go and make disciples of all nations, baptizing them in the Name of the Father, and of the Son, and of the Holy Spirit, and teaching them to obey everything I have commanded you. And surely I will be with you always, to the very end of the age." (Matthew 28:18–20)

The implications of this mandate are revolutionary and have literally altered the course of world history.

Jesus asserts that all authority in heaven is His (see Psalm 103:19). The heights, the depths, the angels, and the principalities are all under His sovereign rule (see Psalm 135:5–7). But all authority on earth is His as well (see Psalm 147:15–18). Man and creature, as well as every invention and institution, are under His providential superintendence (see Psalm 24:1). There are no neutral areas in all the cosmos that can escape His authoritative regency (see Colossians 1:17).

On that basis, Christ says believers all across the wide gulf of time are to continually manifest His Lordship— making disciples in all nations by going, baptizing, and teaching. This mandate is the essence of the New Covenant, which in turn, is just an extension of the Old Covenant: Go and claim everything in heaven and on earth for the everlasting dominion of Jesus Christ (see Genesis 1:26–28).

It was this mandate that originally emboldened those disciples to preach the gospel—first in Jerusalem and Judea, then in Samaria, and finally in the uttermost parts of the earth (see Acts 1:8). It was this mandate that sustained the faithful church through generations of hardship, persecution, calamity, and privation—provoking it to offer light and life to those ensnared in the miry clay of darkness and death. It was this mandate that sent Columbus, Vespucci, Balboa, da Gama, Magellan, and Cabot out across the perilous uncharted seas. And ultimately, it was this mandate that became the catalyst for a remarkable resurgence of missionary efforts—both in word and in deed—that followed on the heels of the great European expansion and colonization during the nineteenth century.

Just as no corner of the globe was left untouched by the explorers, soldiers, merchants, and colonists bearing up under notions of the "White Man's Burden" and "Manifest Destiny," the selfless and sacrificial efforts of missionaries left virtually no stone unturned either. Peoples everywhere tasted their abundant benefits.[8] And, chief among those benefits of course, was a new respect for innocent human life—a respect that was entirely unknown anywhere in the world until the advent of the gospel.

As missionaries moved out from Christendom to the "uttermost parts of the earth," they were shocked to discover all the horrors of untamed heathenism. They found abortion all too prevalent, infanticide all too commonplace, abandonment all too familiar, and euthanasia all too customary. They were confronted by the specters of endemic poverty, recurring famine, unfettered disease, and widespread chattel slavery—which the Christian West had only recently abolished. Cannibalism, ritual abuse, patricide, human sacrifice, sexual perversity, petty tyranny, paternalistic exploitation, live burials, exterminative clan warfare, and genocidal tribal vendettas all predominated.

Again and again, they had to affirm in the clearest possible way—in both word and deed—that Jesus Christ is the only perfect sacrifice for the sins of the world and that through Him had come the death of death (see Romans 5:6–18).

Most of the missionaries knew that such a liberating message would likely be met with strident opposition. And it was. Anna Bowden's experience was by no means unique. Especially toward the end of the great missionary era—during the sunset of Victorianism—missionaries were often forced into conflicts with Europeans and North Americans who subscribed to the Enlightenment notions of Darwinism, Malthusianism, and Eugenics. As these ideas took a higher and higher profile at home, leaders in government and academia—and gradually even in the church—began to increasingly believe that the vast difference between Christian culture and pagan culture was actually not rooted in religion, but in sociology and race. So Christian soldiers stationed in British colonies, for example, were often reprimanded for attending the baptisms of native converts because as representatives of the government, they were obligated to be "religiously neutral." Thus, missionaries found it increasingly difficult to persuade the Western governments to abolish heathen customs and impose the rule of humanitarian law.

Thankfully, the vast majority of the missionaries on the field held the line against such latitudinarianism. They continued to sacrifice. They continued to care for the hurting. They continued to succor the ailing. They continued to value the weak. And they continued to stand for the innocent.

In 1893, a Parliament of Religions was held in Chicago; at hand were delegates from dozens of pagan cults and religious sects from around the world to meet and dialogue with Western church leaders in what organizers called the "universal and trans-religious spirit of cooperation, toleration, and empathy that unites all mankind regardless of its sundry religious impulses."[9] A group of Presbyterian missionaries—representative of thousands of faithful men and women who had seen firsthand the horrors of heathen lands and had sacrificed dearly to bring them help and hope—quenched that spirit with a report that stated succinctly the distinctive appeal of the gospel:

> Just as Buddha, Mohammed, Confucius, Krishna, and Zoroaster remain to this day decayed by irrevocable death, so the religions that bear their names carry with them the stench of the grave. Poverty, barbarity, death, and lasciviousness must be the lot of those men and nations that follow after them. The horrors of children left to die, women sacrificed to dumb idols, and the sick given over to their own devices are the fruit of the flesh that no heathen ravings can be rid. Only the gospel of our Savior Jesus Christ, the Way, the Truth, and the Life, can lend the bequest of life. Only Christ has Himself escaped the shackles of death, and only the faith in Him that comes through grace can free men from the oppressions of the spirit of murder, which we must sadly affirm, is the same as your precious spirit of cooperation, toleration, and empathy.[10]

Another dissenting voice came from a veteran missionary from China who asserted:

> When I reached Amoy thirty-two years ago, there was a pond in the center of town known as the *Babies Pond*. This was the place where unwanted little ones were thrown by their mothers. There were always several bodies of innocents floating on it's green and slimy waters and passersby looked on without surprise. This is what a world without a clear uncompromised Christian gospel leads irrevocably toward.[11]

Still another delegate, a converted Mangaian islander, testified that he had been marked out for ritual sacrifice before the coming of missionaries. By some stroke of Providence, he was temporarily spared. He continued:

> Still I believed that I must die, and in my turn, be offered. But, blessed be Jehovah, not long after the cultus, the gospel was brought to Mangaia. I then learned with wonder that the true peace offering is Jesus, who died

on Calvary, in order that all the wretched slaves of Satan might be freed. This was indeed good news to me. God forbid that we should return to the bondage of universal lawlessness.[12]

Again and again, the faithful concurred; the age-old commitment of the distinctive gospel message must not, can not, and will not be compromised. When it is, not only does heresy sweep through the church, but death sweeps through the land.

To the Uttermost

As missionaries circled the globe, penetrated the jungles, and crossed the seas, they preached a singular message: light out of darkness, liberty out of tyranny, and life out of death. To cultures epidemic with terrible poverty, brutality, lawlessness, and disease, those faithful Christian witnesses interjected the novel Christian concepts of grace, charity, law, medicine, and the sanctity of life. They overturned despots, liberated the captives, and rescued the perishing. They established hospitals. They founded orphanages. They started rescue missions. They built almshouses. They opened soup kitchens. They incorporated charitable societies. They changed laws. They demonstrated love. They lived as if people really mattered.

These kinds of dramatic activities, rather than being isolated occurrences, were actually quite normative. Wherever missionaries went, they faced a dual challenge: confront sin in men's hearts and confront sin in men's cultures. Thus, heroes among their number abound:

- Born to a poor but pious Scottish family in 1813, *David Livingstone* committed his life early on to the work of the gospel. Driven by the dictates of the Great Commission, he went to Africa in 1841 as a missionary-explorer. Going where no white man had ever gone before, Livingstone penetrated the deepest reaches of the conti-

nent proclaiming the good news of Christ. He understood only too well, though, that the purpose of missions extended far beyond merely extending the offer
of heaven to the hapless and hopeless. In his widely
influential book, *Missionary Travels and Researches in
Southern Africa,* he wrote, "The indirect benefits, which
to the casual observer lie beneath the surface and are
inappreciable, in reference to the wide diffusion of
Christianity at some future time, are worth all the
money and labor that have been extended to produce
them."[13] Among those "indirect benefits" in Livingstone's work were the dramatic curtailment of both the
native abortion and slave trades. A legend in his own
time and a paradigm of missionary efficacy ever since,
Livingstone demonstrated the power of the authentic
church in the face of the horrors of heathenism.

- When *Hugh Goldie* joined a mission station in Old
  Calabar on the West Coast of Africa early in the nineteenth century, he was horrified by many of the things
  he found there. The living conditions of the people
  were utterly deplorable. Their nutrition was abomin-
  able. Their hygiene was disgraceful. Their social and
  commercial arrangements were in utter disarray. But it
  was their cavalier attitude to the sanctity of human life
  that most disturbed him. Although they had recently
  abandoned the centuries-old practice of human sacrifice, they still freely practiced abortion, abandonment,
  and infanticide. Goldie was met with stiff opposition by
  the tribal chiefs—and even by many of his fellow missionaries who felt that his pro-life convictions would
  compromise their evangelistic efforts. He stood firmly
  on the integrity of the whole counsel of God. Finally, as
  a result of his lifelong crusade for life, tribal decrees in
  1851 and 1878 banned the terrible customs. He went
  on to his eternal reward having "run the race, fought
  the fight, and held the course" (2 Timothy 4:7).

- *Joseph Damien de Veuster* was born in the lowlands of Bel-
  gium in 1840. After posting a promising academic record, he disappointed his family's expectations of a

brilliant professional career in business, law, or politics
by submitting to a call to the mission field. Assigned to
the newly reopened islands of Hawaii, he served as a
pastor in the burgeoning village of Honolulu for nearly
a decade. His concern for the sanctity of all human life
led him not only to fight against the few remaining
abortionists among the natives, but to eventually re-
quest a transfer to the wretched leprosarium on
Molakai. There, Father Damien—as he came to be
known—helped the people to build homes, schools,
roads, civic halls, and treatment clinics. He protected
the integrity of each resident from persecution and re-
jection, both from within and without the colony. Encouraging the essential Christian values of faith, family,
and work, he helped restore dignity, hope, and purpose to the despised and rejected. His sacrificial character was soon lauded around the globe. Even the renowned literary skeptic, Robert Louis Stevenson, was
struck by Father Damien's saintly service to the unwanted and actually risked his fortune and his reputation by publishing a defense of the great man. Eventually contracting leprosy himself, Father Damien died at
the age of forty-nine. On his tombstone were engraved
the words, "Died a Martyr of Charity."

- Still gripped by a recalcitrant paganism in the nineteenth century, Japan was inhospitable to the gospel
and its proponents. Even so, a handful of pioneer missionaries persevered and bore fruit in the midst of terribly difficult circumstances. The life and ministry of *Jai
Ishii* was just such fruit. Born into a powerful and influential samurai family, he was converted to the faith in
1884 as a teenager at a Presbyterian mission school. Inspired by a visit of George Müeller two years later, Ishii
committed his life to caring for the myriads of abandoned and neglected children that roamed Japan's medieval provinces. His courage and valor in standing
against the tide of the culture became so widely heralded that guilds of abortionists regularly contracted
with assassins to take his life. More often than not, how-

ever, Ishii was able to vanquish his foes—not with power or by might but with the gospel. Eventually, the orphanage, school, and hospital which he founded grew to the point that they housed nearly three hundred children at a time, provided primary health care for the entire feudal region, and asserted the principal outlet of higher culture in all of Okayama. His ministry became a paradigm of Christian compassion and faithfulness in the midst of an emerging Japanese prowess as well as the model the government used—and still uses—in providing legal protection to the unwanted and the rejected.

- At the age of twenty-seven, *Mary Reed* left her family home in Ohio for a life of missionary endeavors on the subcontinent of Asia. Just three years later, after an exhausting tour of ministry among poor low-caste Hindus, she was diagnosed as having leprosy. Clinging to the promises of Scripture concerning the good providence of God, she resolved to redouble her efforts on behalf of the "untouchables." For several years she directed a concerted campaign against *immolation* and *sarti* from a quarantined sick bed. Later, after it became apparent that her disease had gone into complete remission, she launched a dramatic crusade against abortion and abandonment that involved the development of an "underground railroad," a network of sheltering homes, and mobile medical teams providing pre-natal and gynecological care to the needy. When she died in 1899, she left behind a legacy of care that gradually became codified into law throughout the vast Maharashtra province west of Bombay in southern India.

- Kidnapped by Muslim slave-traders from his Yoruba homeland in north-central Africa, *Samuel Adjai Crowther* was rescued by missionaries and baptized into the church in 1825. Six months after acquiring a rudimentary alphabet card, he had taught himself to read the New Testament. His extraordinary intellectual gifts and spiritual initiative became further evident five years later when he was admitted into the Fourah Bay College at the top of his class; within a few months he even became a tutor there. He was part of the first Niger expedition which the British undertook, partly for the sake of geographical knowledge, but also in order to end the slave trade in that region. In 1864, Crowther was consecrated in Canterbury Cathedral as the Missionary Bishop of the Niger Territory. That same year Oxford awarded him a Doctor of Divinity degree. Throughout his life he was an ardent and successful opponent of slavery, human sacrifice, infanticide, and other traditional African customs. After his death in 1891, a fellow-missionary testified that through Bishop Crowther's labor "the horrible slave trade received a great check; the practice of human sacrifice is at an end within the Niger country, and the neighboring chiefs find themselves unable to procure slaves to be immolated by their priests. Instead of the indolence which accompanies the easy gains of the slave-dealer, commerce, with its attendant activity, has had to flee far up the rivers."[14]

- From 1796 to 1820, *Henry Bicknell* served with the London Missionary Society on the Pacific island of Tahiti. There his earnest labors—preaching the gospel and teaching the precepts of faithful living—bore abundant fruit. For years his efforts to legally protect the lives of innocents were met with frustration, however, due to the reign of King Pompare. The Tahitian king was renowned for his bloodthirsty indulgence in human sacrifice. During the thirty years of his rule, he commanded the ritual deaths of more than two thousand of his subjects. Regardless of the occasion—whether it was preparation for war, the consecration of a funeral, or the launching of a canoe—the pagan king insisted on offering a human sacrifice. Bicknell's unflagging efforts to rescue the innocent just before the lethal ceremonies and his uncompromising witness before the throne, ultimately won the king over. Pompare converted and was baptized in 1819. Before the diligent and dedicated missionary died the following year, he helped the once-murderous king frame Christian laws prohibiting abortion, infanticide, abandonment, and euthanasia.

- In 1869, *Friedrich Ramseyer* and his wife Victoria, went to be missionaries at Kumassi on the west coast of Africa. Because their preaching was perceived to be a threat to the Narideggi chieftain, Prempeh and his hoard of witchdoctors, the couple was kidnapped and held for four years. Finally rescued in 1874, the Ramseyers left Africa to recover in England. For twenty-two years, the Ramseyers prayed that God would provide a way for them to return. Meanwhile, the denizens of Kumassi groaned under the oppression of the bloodthirsty king. Prempeh made a practice of killing a slave each night following a lavish feast, solely for his own perverse entertainment. Once a year during a festival of yams, he immolated six hundred of his subjects in a grisly celebration. He had even gone so far as to slaughter four hundred virgins in order to give the walls of his palace a rich red color by mixing their innocent blood with the mortar. Yielding to the Ramseyers' incessant lobbying and cajoling, the British returned to the region in 1895. They immediately deposed the tyrant-king. Soon after, the residents of Kumassi welcomed the missionaries back as long-departed friends, where they worked for another twelve years restructuring the Narideggi society and developing an indigenous law code that would, at long last, fully respect the sanctity of life.

- "Expect great things from God, attempt great things for God" was the famous principle of action first enunciated by the pioneer English missionary, *William Carey*. Serving as both village pastor and cobbler, in 1792 he wrote *An Inquiry into the Obligations of Christians to Use Means for the Conversion of the Heathens* as a response to the popular pseudo-Calvinism of the day—which held that God would convert the lost when He wished and that nothing men did could possibly alter His timing. That book became the catalyst for a number of new evangelistic endeavors. When the Baptist Missionary Society was formed later that same year, he became its first missionary, leaving almost immediately for India. Carey's remarkable work in literacy training and Bible translation proved to be innovative, efficient, and fruit-ful—serving as a model for many missions agencies to this day. But he did not limit his efforts to academic work alone. He quickly discovered that India's long-standing legal tradition gave parents the right to kill their children—a right commonly claimed, especially in the case of infant girls. Even the various Hindu sects that forbade the taking of animal life permitted the murder of newborn daughters. Carey went on an all-out campaign to persuade the British government to outlaw the barbaric practice, and ultimately, despite fierce opposition, he succeeded. Shortly before his death, he personally drafted the reform legislation that prohibited child sacrifice at the yearly festival at Gunga Saugor. And, even now, the statute criminalizing infanticide is called the "Carey Edict."

- *Nan Mullins* was a dedicated and effective Southern Baptist missionary to China. But, in the era of the great model Baptist missionaries like Lottie Moon and Annie Armstrong, Nan was a real enigma. She did not seem to adhere to the standard rules for single women out on the mission field. She eschewed western-style cloth-ing, for instance, having been influenced by J. Hudson Taylor's ideas. In addition, she did not hesitate to ex-tend her ministry beyond the traditional bounds of teaching and nursing—believing that personal evange-lism, discipleship, and social activism were integral to her call. Chief among her concerns was the low regard for life among the rural Chinese. Female infanticide was especially prominent. For eight years Nan labored among the people, caring for them and bearing testi-mony to the basic tenants of the Scriptures. It was not until she lay on her deathbed, however, that the re-gional governor in Nanchung yielded to her lifelong desire: criminalizing all forms of child-killing. He granted it he said, because "All her life Miss Mullins lived selflessly for our people. If I could restore her to health and life, I would. But since I cannot, I will give her what I know she desires even more: health and life for others."[15]

The list of nineteenth century missionaries who fought for the rights and the lives of the innocents is virtually as long as the list of all the missionaries during that era. They comprise a veritable who's who of missions: Nathaniel Forsyth (d. 1813), Joshua Marshman (d. 1837), Henry Martin (d. 1812), Francis Mason (d. 1874), John Newton (d. 1891), Bishop Robert Caldwell (d. 1891), William George Tozer (d. 1899), Charles W. Forman (d. 1894), Andrew T. Pratt (d. 1872), and Thomas Carthen (d. 1896).

Because these faithful men and women were willing to sacrifice their all-in-all for the cause of righteousness, whole cultures were transformed. Besides education, health care, sanitation, economic development, transportation, and communication, missionaries brought a humanitarian law code—rooted not in humanism but in Christian orthodoxy—to the four corners of the earth. The result was that civilization—the comfortable, equitable, and responsible kind of civilization that so many in the West have come to take for granted—was extended anywhere and everywhere that the gospel was given free reign. Interestingly, the converse has also proven to be true: wherever the church has been inhibited, awful reversals in the quality of life have occurred and the innocent have suffered.

Conclusion

When the good news of salvation in Christ first resounded around the Mediterranean world, not only were souls won and lives changed, but the very structure of society was affected—the Roman Empire was turned on its head. As the church's evangelism spread Christendom throughout Europe and the East during the Medieval epoch, not only was personal redemption wrought, but a whole new cultural apparatus was established. Similarly, when the Reformation and the various other reform movements swept across the land, not only were men, women, and children snatched from the jaws of the second death, but they were snatched from the jaws of the first death as well. So it is not surprising to find that during the nineteenth century, when the church launched its greatest missionary effort to date, that the pattern held true to form. And as before, this pattern was rooted in five basic principles:

Orthodoxy

An unfettered, untainted, and uncompromised gospel message had great efficacy on the mission field. As long as the missionaries held to orthodoxy they were able to have success—both in the establishment of Christian communities and in the eradication of pagan brutalities—wherever it was that they were called to minister. It was only when Enlightenment ideas hindered the full application of God's sovereign lordship, that the church was ineffectual in defending the life and liberty of the innocents.

The Church

Missionaries were sent by churches to plant churches. They were not simply relief workers or humanitarian volunteers. They were ambassadors of the church; thus, all their efforts for the poor, the downtrodden, and the oppressed were simply extensions of their sacramental calling. Their pro-life activities were simply manifestations of the fact that the church is called to be a refuge, a shelter, and a sanctuary to those who are being dragged off to death.

Servanthood

To be a missionary has always meant living a life of sacrifice. In the nineteenth century, it also meant leaving behind a life of comfort and ease for the terrifying uncertainties of the howling wilderness. It meant establishing schools and founding hospitals. And it meant facing the horrors of death and destruction. All for the sake of the poor and needy—those who do not know the hope of Christ—that is the essence of ethical servanthood.

Urgency

When souls are lost or babies are killed or women are sacrificed or the elderly are abused or the innocent are enslaved, there is no time to waste. That is why the journals of so many of the missionaries of the nineteenth century are filled with a sense of urgency. That is why so many of them were willing to risk their very lives for the integrity of the church and for the sanctity of life.

Patience

More often than not, the missionaries of the nineteenth century gave their lives to the propagation of the gospel and the promulgation of the pro-life ethic. They knew that theirs was a multi-generational task. And so they patiently gave—thirty, forty, and fifty years—knowing that they would ultimately reap thirty-, sixty-, and a hundred-fold.

      ða   ða   ða

The line remained unbroken. The great pro-life legacy—that had been handed down from the Patristic church to the Medieval church to the Renaissance church—was honored, upheld, and even extended by the missionaries that circled the planet during the nineteenth century. As a result, the foundations of the modern era were laid on the simple contention that human lives matter. If we continue to enjoy the mercies and forbearance of God, it is due to that.

6

LIFE AND LIBERTY:
THE AMERICAN EXPERIENCE
alea iacta est [1]

> *The accursed everyday life of the modernist is instinct with the four
> sins crying to heaven for vengeance, and there is no humanity in it,
> and no simplicity, and no recollection.*
>
> Hilaire Belloc

> *The Modern world is full of the old Christian virtues gone mad. The
> virtues have gone mad because they have been isolated from each
> other and are wandering alone. Thus some scientists care for truth;
> but their truth is pitiless. And thus some humanitarians care only
> for pity; but their pity—I am sorry to say—is often untruthful.*
>
> G. K. Chesterton

n July 1871, Augustus St. Clair was given an extremely dangerous undercover investigative assignment for the *New York Times*: he was to infiltrate and ultimately expose the city's prosperous and profligate *medical malpractice* industry—the common euphemism for the abortion trade.

For several weeks, he and a "lady friend" visited a number of the most heavily trafficked clinics in New York, posing as a couple facing a crisis pregnancy. They were shocked with what they saw.

It wasn't that the clinics were sordid back-alley affairs. They weren't. It wasn't that they were operated by shady or seedy quacks. They weren't. It wasn't that they were dark, dangerous, and disreputable. They weren't.

On the contrary, it was that the rich splendor of the entrepreneurial abortuaries—fine tapestry carpets, expensive mahogany furniture, elegant decorations, and spacious parlors—contrasted so sharply with the desperation, helplessness, and poverty of their clientele. It was that the smug complacency of the poisonous proprietors—men and women who made quite an opulent living out of dying—contrasted so sharply with the dispiritedness of their patients. It was that the frank and forthright commerce of the death merchants—advertised openly in all the magazines, newspapers, digests of the day—contrasted so sharply with the secretive shame of their customers. It was that the dens of iniquity were simultaneously dens of inequity.

As a result of his sordid discoveries, St. Clair wrote a hard-hitting three-column article which the *Times* published in late August. Entitled "The Evil of the Age," the article opened with a solemn warning:

> The enormous amount of *medical malpractice* that exists and flourishes, almost unchecked, in the city of New York, is a theme for most serious consideration. Thousands of human beings are thus murdered before they have seen the light of this world, and thousands upon thousands more of adults are irremediably robbed in constitution, health, and happiness.[2]

Skillfully, St. Clair portrayed virtually every dimension of the slick and professional abortion industry: from its bottom-line economics to its medical methodologies, from its marketing savvy to its litigal invulnerability. Told with passion and insight, the story hit the city like a bombshell. Almost singlehandedly, the young reporter put abortion on the public agenda for the first time in decades.[3]

Being on the public agenda is not enough in itself to bring about widespread social change, however. Something more is needed—an incident to galvanize the concern of the public. In the good providence of God, just such an incident occurred in New York just days after St. Clair's article appeared in the *Times*.

The body of a beautiful young woman was discovered inside an abandoned trunk in a railway station baggage room. A police autopsy determined that the cause of death was a botched abortion.

The *Times* provided stark details:

> This woman, a full five feet in height, had been crammed into a trunk two feet six inches long. Seen even in this position and rigid in death, the young girl, for she could not have been more than eighteen, had a face of singular loveliness. But her chief beauty was her great profusion of golden hair, that hung in heavy folds over her shoulders, partly shrouding her face. There was no mark of violence upon the body, although there was some discoloration and decomposition about the pelvic region. It was apparent that here was a new victim of man's lust, and the life destroying arts of those abortionists, whose practices have lately been exposed.[4]

For several days, readers were spellbound as the tragic story began to unfold. They followed the tortured movements of detectives and investigators with horrified fascination. The chain of events was carefully retraced. The young girl was identified. Her seducer—who had made the clandestine arrangements for her fatal surgery—was revealed. Even the perpetrator of the wretched crime was tracked down.

When at last the suspect was apprehended—a prominent Fifth Avenue physician named Dr. Rosenzweig—the entire city was startled once again by St. Clair's revelations. During his investigations the previous month, he had actually interviewed Rosenzweig in the doctor's office:

As we entered the room a young girl emerged there-
from. She seemed to be about twenty years of age, a little
more than five feet in height, of slender build, having
blue eyes, and a clear, alabaster complexion. Long
blonde curls, tinted with gold, drooped upon her shoul-
ders, and her face wore an expression of embarrassment
at the presence of strangers. She retreated to the end of
the hall, and stood there for a moment, and then went
to another part of the house. In a few moments . . .[5]

He went on to describe his conversation with
Rosenzweig. The doctor was more than candid about the
arrangements and proceeded to quote a flat fee of two
hundred dollars—quite a sum in that time. When St. Clair
asked about the aborted child, the doctor replied:

"Don't worry about that, my dear sir. I will take care of
the result. A newspaper bundle, a basket, a pail, a resort
to the sewer, or the river at night? Who is the wiser?"[6]

When St. Clair persisted with his questioning,
Rosenzweig suddenly became suspicious and indignant, vio-
lently driving the reporter off the premises at pistol point.
As he made his retreat, he caught a final glimpse of the
doctor's office:

As I passed through the hallway I saw the same girl who
had left the parlor when I made my first visit to the
house. She was standing on the stairs, and it was the
same face I saw afterward in the morgue. I positively
identify the features of the dead woman as those of the
blonde beauty before described.[7]

St. Clair's boldness was not without risk. Abortion was
big business. And abortionists were men and women of
great power and influence. They attempted to pressure the
young reporter and his editors at the *Times*—with veiled
threats, proffered bribes, and political innuendo—to back
away from his story.[8] They were even able to put into motion the forces of the infamous and corrupt machine at
Tammany Hall.[9]

Still, at the risk of his reputation, his life, and his career, St. Clair stood his ground. His commitment to the sanctity of life—growing out of his Dutch Reformed Church heritage—remained steadfast.[10] His courage stood out in an age alternately mesmerized by a vertigo of indifference and charmed by a platonic insomnia. In fact, his courage became an unforeseen catalyst far more meaningful than its didactic pretext.

How the West Was Won

Like an avowed atheist who sees the devil at night, America awoke in a jolt to the horror of abortion. Suddenly—like the flash of Lavoisier's mirror or the sweep of Foucault's pendulum—concern over the scandal of child-killing became something more than grist for journalism's mill. It became a moral crusade. It became a movement; an outcry against the insidious exploitation of women and children swept the nation.

At first, the press was disinclined to expose the homicidal details of the abortion industry due to the possibility of their own loss of income—abortionists accounted for as much as a quarter of all classified advertising dollars for a number of local newspapers. But a number of courageous journalists, following St. Clair's lead in the *Times,* began to expose the awful practices of heretofore respectable and upstanding physicians, who traded on the misfortunes of others. Before long, the dam of self-interest broke and a flood of articles began to appear in several other New York papers—the *Tribune,* the *Herald,* and the *Police Gazette.* Soon, all around the country, the same newspapers, magazines, and digests that had previously accepted advertising from abortionists began to throw the searchlight of truth on their detestable deeds of darkness—in New Orleans, in San Francisco, in Philadelphia, in Boston, in Washington, in Cleveland, and in innumerable other cities. Sensational headlines began to appear in profusion: "The Crime

Against Nature," "A Damnable Deed," "The Curse of American Society," "The Terrible Sins Which Vanity and Fashion Lead Their Devotees to Commit," "A Long Record of Infamy," "Child Murder in Massachusetts," and "The Demon Doctor."[11]

Though the medical community was still fragmented, disorganized, and disconnected, virtually every professional medical association began to decry any and all forms of child-killing. The fledgling American Medical Association, for instance, circulated a gynecological report emphasizing the necessity of protecting "the safety of the child" at all times, and denouncing "the perverted views of morality" underlying abortion.[12] It resolved to expel from its ranks all abortionists—who were but "modern Herods," "educated assassins," and "monsters of iniquity," who presented "a hideous view of moral deformity as the evil spirit could present."[13] The organization's professional periodical, the *Journal of the American Medical Association,* published a scathing critique of abortion's death ethic noting that from the moment of conception:

> The unborn child is human, and at all periods differs in degree and not in kind from the infant and the adult. Therefore, we must regard it as a human being with an inalienable right to life, and that its destruction is homicide.[14]

Even reticent politicians and barristers began to take notice and to take action.[15] Tougher restrictive legislation, more efficient local enforcement, and strict sentencing guidelines were put into place all around the country, and the prosperous physician-killers were driven to desperate resources. Eventually every state in the Union passed laws making their morbid arts illegal. Many went so far as to affirm that the abortion of "any woman pregnant with child is an assault with intent to murder."[16] With penalties ranging from seven years of hard labor in the penitentiary to life in prison, the crime was clearly and legally vilified.[17]

But as impressive as all these efforts were—in the press, in the medical community, and in the political arena—it was the church that led the pro-life movement toward a consummate victory.

Actually, the nineteenth century American church seemed uniquely impotent to lead such an important struggle. The Catholic community was still largely comprised of immigrants and was thus excluded from the mainstream of American discourse. And the divisive moral and political dilemma of chattel slavery dominated the thinking of most Protestants—to the exclusion of almost everything else—in both the North and the South. But for many, the ironic similarities between the abortion issue and the slavery issue could not be ignored. And so, a number of courageous pioneers shook the church out of its doldrums. Once again, they were able to place the issue of abortion squarely before the people.

The Catholic bishops of Baltimore, Boston, and New York issued strong statements reiterating the church's historic commitment to protect innocent human life around mid-century. Then, when Pope Pius IX renewed the medieval censures against abortion in 1869, each local parish was encouraged in an encyclical to become involved in pro-life activity:

> To serve the least of our brethren is the substance and the essence of our earthly duties, thus portraying in the plainest fashion the gospel of grace; therefore, let all attend to the protection of the unwanted child as much as the sickly neighbor. For such as this shall we all be called unto account.[18]

Methodist and Baptist churches, shortly after the War Between the States, began widely circulating several pro-life sermon booklets, including Indiana minister E. Frank Howe's classic *A Sermon on Ante-Natal Infanticide*. The booklets showed that the Bible teaches that life begins at conception—in more than forty different passages from

Genesis to Revelation—and that abortion is thus "no less than murder."[19]

In 1868, a conference of the Congregationalist churches issued a stinging denunciation of abortion and its shockingly wide prevalence. It urged faithful believers to stand firm in their Scriptural convictions in the strongest possible terms:

> Let imagination draw the darkest picture that reason or taste could allow, and it would fail to set forth adequately the outlines and shocking details of this practice. Our investigation has brought us to the belief that after all the proper deductions, full one third of the natural population of our land, fails by the hand of violence; that in no one year of the late war have so many lost life in camp or battle, as have failed of life by reason of this horrid home crime. We shudder to view the horrors of intemperance, of slavery, and of war; but those who best know the facts and bearing of this crime, declare it to be a greater evil, more demoralizing and destructive, than either intemperance, slavery, or war itself.[20]

The report went on to prophetically condemn the lascivious and concupiscent lifestyles that drove young men and women to such extremes:

> Fashion, inexorable, tyrannical, with its whirl of amusements and frivolous enjoyments, has come to demand of religion not only, but of nature herself, that they bend to her despotism, and sacrifice on her bloody altar. A low love of pleasure and ease, vitiated tastes, perverted views of life, and ruined moral sentiments have so wrought themselves into our civilization as a low and vicious leaven, that we have come to consent to customs and habits that will destroy us as a people inevitably, unless arrested betimes.[21]

In a similar fashion, the Presbyterian churches adopted a stridently pro-life position at their general assembly in 1869:

This assembly regards the destruction by parents of their own offspring, before birth, with abhorrence, as a crime against God and against nature; and as the frequency of such murders can no longer be concealed, we hereby warn those that are guilty of this crime that, except they repent, they cannot inherit eternal life. We also exhort those that have been called to preach the gospel, and all who love purity and truth, and who would avert the just judgments of Almighty God from the nation, that they be no longer silent, or tolerant of these things, but that they endeavor by all proper means to stay the floods of impurity and cruelty.[22]

Besides the fiery evangelist D. L. Moody, perhaps the most popular preacher in America immediately following the war was the Congregationalist John Todd. In 1867, he added his voice to the groundswell of pro-life sentiment in an article entitled "Fashionable Murder." In an interview sometime later, he reiterated the importance of the issue:

Murder is, of course, heinous of its own accord. But the murder of a mother's own flesh within the womb is a crime against heaven that is the very essence of sin and inimicable with the Christian religion. Left alone, such a crime would sunder the whole fabric of our families, of our communities, of our churches, of our markets and industries, and finally of our nation. We have rid ourselves of the blight of Negro slavery, affirming that no man may be considered less than any other man. Now let us apply that holy reason to the present scandal.[23]

Summarizing the overall response of the Christian community to the abortion issue, Arthur Cleveland Cox, the renowned Episcopal bishop of the diocese of New York, said that:

Though physicians and journalists have laid much of the groundwork for the exposure of this awful crime against God and man, it was the Christian churches, all of the churches across the broad spectrum of denomination and sect, that have brought hope and help to the innocents. For a glittering moment, I have seen Christ's Body as one.[24]

So monolithic was the consensus that the church forged, that even the most ardent feminists had to rally under the pro-life banner. Susan B. Anthony, for instance, declared:

> I deplore the horrible crime of child murder. We must reach the root of the evil. It is practiced by those whose inmost souls revolt from dreadful need. No matter what the motive, love of ease, or a desire to save from suffering the unborn innocent, the woman is awfully guilty who commits the deed; but oh, thrice guilty is he who drove her to the desperation which impelled her to the crime.[25]

Elizabeth Cady Stanton agreed:

> When we consider that women are often treated as property, it is degrading to women all the more that we should treat our children as property to be disposed of as we see fit.[26]

As did Matilda Gage:

> This subject lies deeper down into woman's wrongs than any other. But, the crime of abortion is not one in which the guilt lies soley [sic] with the woman. Indeed, I hesitate not to assert that most of this crime of child murder, abortion, or infanticide, lies at the door of all men.[27]

In less than two decades, the church was able to marshall hostile journalists, ambivalent physicians, reticent politicians, and even radical feminists to the cause of exploited mothers and their helpless unborn. They succeeded overwhelmingly. And they restored the foundations of a glorious legacy of freedom and justice that had always been at the heart of the remarkable American experiment.

Law and Life

The great liberties that have been enjoyed in America over two hundred years of history were secured against the arbitrary and fickle whims of men and movements by *the rule of law.* The American system of government has not depended upon the benevolence of the magistrates or the altruism of the wealthy or the condescension of the powerful. Every citizen, rich or poor, man or woman, native-born or immigrant, hale or handicapped, young or old, has been considered equal under the standard of unchanging, immutable, and impartial justice.

As Thomas Paine wrote in *Common Sense,* the powerful booklet that helped spark the War for Independence, "In America, the law is king."[28]

If left to the mere discretion of human authorities, all statutes, edicts, and ordinances inevitably devolve into tyranny. There must therefore be an absolute against which no encroachment of prejudice or preference may interfere. There must be a foundation that the winds of change and the waters of circumstance cannot erode. There must be a basis for law that can be depended upon at all times, in all places, and in every situation.

Apart from this Christian innovation in the affairs of men, there can be no freedom. There never has been before, and there never will be again. The Founding Fathers of the American republic knew that only too well.

The opening refrain of the Declaration of Independence affirms the necessity of an absolute standard upon which the rule of law must be based:

> We hold these truths to be self-evident, that all men are created equal; that they are endowed by their Creator with certain inalienable rights; that among these are life, liberty, and the pursuit of happiness. That, to secure these rights, governments are instituted among men, deriving their just powers from the consent of the governed.

Appealing to the "Supreme Judge of the World" for guidance, and relying on His "Divine Providence" for wisdom, the framers committed themselves and their posterity to the absolute standard of "the laws of nature and nature's God." And the essence of that standard, they said, were the inalienable, God-given, and sovereignly endowed rights of *life, liberty,* and *the pursuit of happiness.* A just government exists, they argued, solely and completely to "provide guards" for the "future security" of that essence. Take it away, and the rule of law is no longer possible.

Thomas Jefferson asserted that, "The chief purpose of government is to protect life. Abandon that and you have abandoned all."[29]

Abraham Lincoln pressed the same issue home when he questioned the institution of slavery on the basis of the sanctity of all human life and the rule of law:

> I should like to know if taking this old Declaration of Independence, which declares that all men are equal upon principle, and making exceptions to it, where it will stop. If one man says it does not mean a Negro, why not another say it does not mean some other man?[30]

Because the commercial promoters of abortion were so diligent in their assault on the unborn, the aged, and the infirmed, the rule of law in the nineteenth century was thrown into very real jeopardy. No one was absolutely secure, because absoluteness was thrown out of the constitutional vocabulary. Because the right to life was abrogated for at least some citizens, *all* the liberties of *all* the citizens were at risk because suddenly arbitrariness, relativism, and randomness entered the legal equation. The checks against petty partiality and blatant bias were disabled.

That was hardly the rule of law. Instead, it was the brutal imposition of fashion and fancy by privileged interlopers. It was the denial of everything that the great American experiment in liberty had thus far stood for. Left unchecked, it surely would have been the harbinger of the *end* of that experiment.

Thomas Jefferson even acknowledged as much, saying:

> Can the liberties of a nation be sure when we remove their only firm basis, a conviction in the minds of the people, that these liberties are the gift of God? That they are not to be violated but with his wrath? Indeed, I tremble for my country, when I reflect that God is just; that His justice cannot sleep forever, that revolution of the wheel of fortune, a change of situation, is among possible events; that it may become probable by supernatural influence! The Almighty has no attribute which can take side with us in that event.[31]

Although these truths have always been "self-evident" in the sense that they are written on the fleshly tablet of every man's heart, they certainly have not always been universally accepted (see Romans 1:19–22). In fact, such reasoning is, to some a "stumbling block," and to others "mere foolishness" (1 Corinthians 1:23). That is because the rule of law is a Christian idea, made possible only by the revelation of law from on high. And all too many nineteenth century Americans attempted to "suppress" that truth in one way, shape, form, or another (Romans 1:18). Thus, the nascent abortion industry in that era.

Protecting Rights

In order to protect and preserve *any* rights, the courageous Christian pro-life leaders—in the press, in medicine, in law, and in the church—recognized that they had to protect and preserve *all* rights, beginning with the fundamental rights of life, liberty, and the pursuit of happiness. But in order to protect *those* rights, they had to return to that distinctly Christian notion that the God who providentially rules the affairs of men has already inalienably endowed them to each of us—and thus that they had to match the rhetoric of liberty with the activity of liberation.

That they did. Their sacrificial efforts demonstrated all too clearly that when words are supported by deeds, there is no stopping the fresh wind of hope:

- *Elizabeth Ann Seton* was born in 1774 to a very prominent New York family. At twenty, she married a professor of anatomy and entered into the cosmopolitan life of ease and privilege. In 1803, her husband died leaving her with five children to raise. Shortly thereafter, she was converted and began seeking tangible ways to express her newfound faith through service. She worked with the poor, the sick, and the distressed for some years before she finally focused on the care of cast-off and abused children. Her efforts to expose the horrors of illicit abortions drew attention to her work and enabled her to effect a number of changes in both legislation and enforcement. When she died in 1821, she left a small community that has continued to propagate her vision up to the present day.

- An upright Presbyterian minister, *Stephen Soyers* epitomized the Christian values and virtues of the antebellum South. A strong opponent of chattel slavery and the oppressive plantation system, he was nonetheless a reluctant supporter of the Confederacy on constitutional grounds. During the War Between the States, the focus of his ministry in central Mississippi was on mercy ministry. He and his wife had an extensive work among the families of victims of the war—the poor, orphans, widows, the disabled, and the dispossessed. When they discovered that a number of midwives and nurse practitioners were performing abortions and dispensing chemical parricides among both the enslaved blacks and free-born whites, they launched a protracted battle against the minions of death. Though he did not survive to see the end of the war, his work continued long after—laying the foundations for Mississippi's strong pro-life legislation passed at the turn of the century.

- *Horatio Robinson Storer* was a third generation Boston physician and a specialist in obstetrics and gynecology. He became concerned about the booming abortion trade in 1855 and immediately sought ways to utilize his family influence to halt the slaughter. He wrote to his friends and contacts in the profession all over the country inquiring about the abortion laws in each of their states. He then began to bombard medical societies and professional journals with information, resolutions, and litigation. He confronted, cajoled, and preached. He lobbied, argued, and prayed. He became the lightning rod for the national debate over abortion. He wrote two widely circulated and popularly lauded books—*Why Not? A Book for Every Woman* and *Is It I? A Book for Every Man*—which detailed the "criminality and physical evils" of child-killing procedures. Clearly, he was the greatest and most influential pro-life advocate of his day. The American Medical Association ultimately appointed him chairman of a select committee to oppose child-killing procedures altogether. And thus was born America's first national right to life organization—as an ancillary of the AMA no less.

- Another doctor who entered the pro-life fray was the venerable *Hugh Hodge,* who was one of the most prominent researchers in the field of embryology in the nineteenth century. He often exhorted his medical students at the University of Pennsylvania to protect innocent human life. His research had convinced him beyond any shadow of a doubt that life began at conception and that the destruction of that life before or after birth was unmitigated murder. In 1854, he began to lobby the American Medical Association, in cooperation with the young Dr. Storer, to call a halt to the slaughter of children in the clinics of the land. Although it took many years, Dr. Hodge never wavered— his faith in Christ bolstered him through every trial— and ultimately he was successful: the AMA strongly denounced the brutal practice in September 1871.

- *Louis Jennings* was a pioneer in American journalism. The editor of the *New York Times* during the last decades of the nineteenth century, he helped to build the reputation of that paper, ultimately making it the premier daily in the entire nation. He was also a committed Christian and a stalwart in the struggle for life. In 1870, Jennings began a crusade against abortion on the editorial pages of his paper that finally lead to the criminalization of the procedure in every state in the Union. He understood the power of the printed page and utilized it expertly. He knew only too well that it would be necessary to provoke a public outrage over the issue, not simply a stiffening of legislation that might go unenforced. It was his leadership, and the national visibility of his paper that ultimately swayed both the legal and the medical establishments to publicly denounce abortion as murder.

- *Leslie Printice* was a young widow in New York City when she first became active in the pro-life movement. A member of Gardiner Spring's congregation at the prominent Brick Presbyterian Church, she was encouraged by his sermons on child-killing to take a bold and active stand. She organized several meetings in her midtown Manhattan brownstone of doctors, lawyers, politicians, judges, and community leaders to hear the facts about the abortion trade. Under the auspices of the church she set up the New York Parent and Child Committee. The committee established prayer networks, sidewalk counseling shifts, and even alternative care programs with Christian doctors. It also organized regular protests in front of Anna Lohman's five area abortion franchises. Known professionally as Madame Restell, Lohman was the boldest, richest, and most visible child-killer. Tenacious and unrelenting, Leslie led a rally outside Lohman's lavish home in 1846 that was by turns emotional, physical, and fierce. When Lohman went to trial for the first time the next year, Leslie was there—despite innumerable threats on her life from a number of the gangsters on Lohman's payroll—to testify with several children "saved from the butcher's knife." Nearly half a century later, her efforts were recognized in Albany by Theodore Roosevelt as the primary catalyst for the state's tougher legislation and stiffer enforcement.

- The *National Police Gazette* was undoubtedly the most sensational newspaper in America. Popular, brash, and controversial, the *Gazette* was edited by *George Wilkes,* a tough veteran of New York City journalism. Though the paper regularly filled three of its eight pages with advertising—including a strong complement from patent medicine manufacturers—Wilkes refused to provide any space to abortionists. He regularly wrote editorials calling for the criminalization of the industry—calling the practitioners of the procedure "human fiends," "professional murderers," and "child destroyers." He chastised officials for not taking stronger action and predicted a "day of vengeance" for all those who stood idly by. While other newspapers were silent, Wilkes continued to awaken consciences; in fact, the prominent pastor Gardiner Spring and the famed editor Louis Jennings would both later credit Wilkes with having provoked them to action.

- Born the youngest of thirteen children in northern Italy, *Frances Cabrini* came to America in 1889 to work among the Italian immigrants of Chicago. In the course of twenty-eight years of ministry there, she established six schools, four hospitals, seven orphanages, two maternity homes, and twenty-three prison outreaches. A woman of extraordinary energy, passion, commitment, and zeal—she lead an educational campaign among immigrant women to help them avoid the pitfalls of abortion and radical feminism. Traveling extensively throughout the continent, she brought her pro-life message of hope in Christ to thousands of thirsty souls.

- In 1856, *Samuel Taylor* was a prototypical mild-mannered small town pharmacist. A family man, community leader, and lifelong Methodist, he had a natural

Midwestern aversion to controversy. But when the daughter of one of his customers was nearly poisoned by a dose of mail-order abortifacient pills, he sprang into action. He discovered that the abortifacient business was booming all over the United States—and that it was an entirely unrestricted, unregulated, and unmonitored industry. Without the benefits of a government agency, an institutional largess, or a corporate sponsor, he began a one-man educational campaign—first with his fellow pharmacists, later expanding to physicians, and finally with state legislators—to alert the public to the physical dangers and the moral liabilities of the child-killing trade. Taylor testified before the Ohio, Illinois, and Indiana legislatures, winning their support for a ban on the sale of all chemical parricides and abortifacients, and he drafted model legislation that was approved by fourteen other states.

- One of the most hated, and at the same time, most admired men in nineteenth century America was *Anthony Comstock*. As a special prosecutor for the U.S. Post Office and director of the New York Society for the Suppression of Vice, he led a lifelong massive anti-obscenity campaign. He was responsible for innumerable legislative initiatives that banned pornography and other sexually explicit materials from the mails. In addition, between 1872 and 1880 he oversaw the arrest and conviction of fifty-five abortionists operating up and down the east coast, including the notorious Anna Lohman. Even after he had relinquished his post, the legislation he had drafted was used to prosecute a number of the abortion industry's stellar personalities from Margaret Sanger, the infamous founder of Planned Parenthood, to Julius Hammer, father of Armand and cofounder of the American Communist Party.

Walking in the footsteps of the innumerable heroes of the faith that had gone before, the pro-life believers of nineteenth century America proclaimed the truth, stood for righteousness, cared for the hurting, sheltered the unwanted, and rescued the perishing. Notable among their number was: Marcus Grady (d. 1879), Zephaniah Swift (d. 1834), Lemuel Whitman (d. 1846), Doris Haddon (d. 1901), Thomas Day (d. 1829), Dr. Thomas Blatchford (d. 1862), Mildred Thompson (1855), Dr. Henry Brisbane (d. 1877), Dr. Alexander Semmes (d. 1871), and Marrisa Letchworth (d. 1913).

Overcoming tremendous obstacles, these faithful pro-life stalwarts transformed the entire ecology of American criminal law. At the outset of the nineteenth century child-killing was actually legal—if only marginally—in every state in the Union. By the end of the century the procedure had been criminalized across the board. Most of the legal changes came during a short twenty-year period from 1860 to 1880. And so once again the message of life and hope overcame and defeated the minions of death and despair.

Conclusion

Like so many times before, the dark specter of death cast a long shadow across the American landscape during the nineteenth century. And like so many times before, faithful followers of Christ rose to the occasion to defend the needy and the helpless with their very all-in-all. At a time when the nation was riven with strife over the recalcitrance of chattel slavery, the proliferation of abortion, and the challenging of the most basic principles of American liberty, they demonstrated in word and deed that every human being is made in the image of God and is thus sacred.

These efforts were rooted in five basic principles:

Orthodoxy

The Christians who put the pro-life movement at the forefront of the national agenda did not do it for the sake of political or institutional expediency. They did not do it for the sake of personal gain or political control. They did it because they believed in the sovereignty of the living God of the Bible. They were rooted in Scriptural orthodoxy and thus knew that in His good providence, God has called on His people to act responsibly, forthrightly, and decisively on behalf of the innocents.

The Church

The popular press made information about abortion available to the average man on the street. The medical associations made physicians aware of the physical risks and the moral compromises inherently involved in the procedure. Lawyers, politicians, and judges enacted the legal constraints necessary to criminalize abortion profiteers. But it was the church that catalyzed and spearheaded the wildly successful pro-life efforts of the nineteenth century.

Servanthood

The pro-life stalwarts of nineteenth century America did not simply say "no" to abortion; they said "yes" to women in crisis. They said "yes" to the poor and desperate. They said "yes" to the confused and afflicted. In short, they fulfilled their servanthood mandate simultaneously with their prophetic mandate.

Urgency

The immediacy and fervency of the Christians during this era is vivid testimony to the fact that they understood the urgency of their task. As long as one abortionist was still plying his grisly trade, as long as one child remained in jeopardy, and as long as one woman was left in the lurch with nowhere to turn, they were unsatisfied. One is one too many. So they acted with sure resolve and with unwavering wholeheartedness, risking everything they had for the sake of those who had nothing to risk.

Patience

Knowing that whatever they did would establish a precedent for generations to come, the doctors, lawyers, and churchmen who led the pro-life cause were careful, cautious, and patient. They wanted to make certain that their efforts would not be in vain. They rested in the security of God's promises and the surety of God's providence.

❧ ❧ ❧

Lives were saved, families restored, and a remarkable foundation of liberty was laid for future generations by the men and women who dedicated themselves to the cause of the sanctity of human life. America at last seemed poised to fulfill her promise—as the land of the free and the home of the brave.

PART 3

THE
THIRD TIME
AROUND

*Human affairs are moved from deep springs.
A spirit moves them. It is by the acceptation,
the denial, and the renewal of philosophies
that this society of immortal mortals is
marked, changed, or restored.*
                Hilaire Belloc

*The great intellectual tradition that comes
down to us from the past was never inter-
rupted or lost through such trifles as the sack
of Rome, the triumph of Attila, or all the barbarian invasions of the Dark Ages. It was lost
after the introduction of printing, the discov-
ery of America, the founding of the Royal Society, and all the enlightenment of the Renaissance and the modern world. It was there, if
anywhere, that there was lost or impatiently
snapped the long thin delicate thread that
had descended from distant antiquity; the
thread of that unusual human hobby: the
habit of thinking.*
                G. K. Chesterton

7

ABOMINATIONS
AND ADMONITIONS:
THE MAKING OF MODERNISM

extinctus amabitur idem [1]

As always happens to miraculous things, the virtue has all gone out with the lapse of time.

Hilaire Belloc

If the world grows too worldly, it can be rebuked by the church; but if the church grows too worldly, it cannot be adequately rebuked for worldliness by the world.

G. K. Chesterton

hen Marx and Engles began their *Communist Manifesto* with the eloquent sentence, "A spector is haunting Europe," they were at least partly right. A spector was indeed haunting Europe; in fact, it was haunting the whole earth. But, it was not the spector that they had imagined. Instead, it was the primal spector of resurgent abortion. It was the aboriginal spector of child-killing.

Some battles just don't stay won. Especially when they are rooted in the very character of fallen man.

Theodore Roosevelt, writing on the eve of America's entry into the First World War in 1917, exhorted his fellow citizens to be on guard against that ancient spector:

> The world is at this moment passing through one of those terrible periods of convulsion when the souls of men and of nations are tried as by fire. Woe to the man or to the nation that at such a time stands as once Laodicea stood; as the people of ancient Meroz stood, when they dared not come to the help of the Lord against the mighty. In such a crisis the moral weakling is the enemy of the right, the enemy of life, liberty, and the pursuit of happiness.[2]

That was a remarkable warning from a remarkable man—a man of unbounded energies and many careers. Before his fiftieth birthday, Roosevelt had served as a New York state legislator, the under-secretary of the Navy, police commissioner for the city of New York, U.S. civil service Commissioner, the governor of New York, vice-president under William McKinley, a colonel in the U.S. Army, and two terms as the president of the United States. In addition, he had written nearly thirty books, run a cattle ranch in the Dakota Territories, and conducted scientific expeditions on four continents. He was a brilliant man who read at least five books every week of his life. He was a physical man who enjoyed hunting, boxing, and wrestling. He was a spiritual man who took his faith very seriously and for years taught Sunday school in his Dutch Reformed Church. And he was a family man who lovingly raised five children and enjoyed a lifelong romance with his wife.

He was, indeed, a remarkable man.

And he lived in a remarkable time—at the sunset of one century and the dawning of another.

The United States had grown from sixteen states in 1800 to forty-five in 1900, from nine hundred thousand square miles to almost four million, and from a population of five million to seventy-six million. That century had produced steamships, railroads, streetcars, bicycles, rollerskates, the air brake, the torpedo, telephones, telegraphs, transatlantic cables, harvesting machines, threshers, cotton gins, cooking ranges, sewing machines, phonographs, typewriters, electric lights, illuminating gas, photographs, x-rays, motion pictures, and cottonseed oil. According to journalist Edward Byrn, the comparison of the start of the century with the end of the century was "like the juxtaposition of a distant star with the noonday sun."[3] And popular historian M. J. de Forest Shelton exclaimed in all truthfulness that there was "more difference between Napoleon's day and ours than between Napoleon's and Julius Caesar's. One century against eighteen."[4] Agreeing, the English intellectual Frederic Harrison, said:

> Take it all in all, the merely material, physical, mechanical change in human life in the hundred years, from the days of Watt and Arkwright to our own, is greater than occurred in the thousand years that preceded, perhaps even the two thousand or twenty thousand years.[5]

Despite bitter labor agitation, anarchist strikes, communist insurgencies, and the emergence of terrorism as a political weapon; despite attempts on the lives of the Prince of Wales, the German Emperor, and the Shah of Persia; despite successful assassinations of King Umberto of Italy and President McKinley; despite the uproar of the Dreyfus affair in France and the Robida scandal in Austria; despite the imminent passing of the old world order—and its accompanying spector—*despite everything*, a robust optimism pervaded the thinking of most Westerners. Their advances, after all, had been stunning. So, for the most part, they shared the opinion of the *New York World* in its prediction that the new century would "meet and overcome all perils and prove to be the best that this steadily improving planet has ever seen."[6]

Theodore Roosevelt had a saner view, a more realistic view of his time. It was a view balanced by a Christian understanding of mankind—made in the very image of God but, at the same time, fallen. With penetrating perception and prophetic precision, he said:

> Progress has brought us both unbounded opportunities and unbridled difficulties. Thus, the measure of our civilization will not be *that* we have done much, but *what* we have done with that much. I believe that the next half century will determine if we will advance the cause of Christian civilization or revert to the horrors of brutal paganism. The thought of modern industry in the hands of Christian charity is a dream worth dreaming. The thought of industry in the hands of paganism is a nightmare beyond imagining. The choice between the two is upon us.[7]

He saw all too clearly the dangers that faced the Western world as it marched so boldly, so confidently into the twentieth century. That is why he devoted himself to remedying as many of those dangers as he possibly could throughout his life. His reforms focused on the needs of the poor working man, on the struggling immigrant, on the miserable tenement dweller, on the helpless widow and orphan, and on the pioneering homesteader. But above all else, his reforms focused on the needs of the *ordinary* family—which was facing *extraordinary* new pressures and changes. In his State of the Union message in 1905, he underscored this priority saying:

> The transformation of the family is one of the greatest sociological phenomena of our time; it is a social question of the first importance, of far greater importance than any merely political or economic question can be.[8]

He went on to describe his simple agenda for protecting the family against the encroachment of those men and women he called "the foes of our own household." He said:

> There are those who believe that a new modernity demands a new morality. What they fail to consider is the harsh reality that there is no such thing as a new moral-

ity. There is only one morality. All else is immorality. There is only true Christian ethics over against which stands the whole of paganism. If we are to fulfill our great destiny as a people, then we must return to the old morality, the sole morality.[9]

His analysis was sterling:

All these blatant sham reformers, in the name of a new morality, preach the old, old vice of self-indulgence which rotted out first the moral fiber and then even the external greatness of Greece and Rome.[10]

It is not surprising then, that when a new wave of abortion advocates made their way onto the American scene and into the public arena, Roosevelt was one of their chief opponents; in fact, apart from the hierarchy of the Catholic church, he was one of their *only* opponents.[11]

He railed against their "frightful and fundamental immorality," calling their cause a submission "to coldness, to selfishness, to love of ease, to shrinking from risk, and to an utter and pitiful failure in sense of perspective."[12] But he did not simply hurl invectives their way—he *acted.* As he said:

The foes of our own household are our worst enemies; and we can oppose them, not only by exposing them and denouncing them, but by constructive work in planning and building reforms which shall take into account both the economic and the moral factors in human advance. We in America can attain our great destiny only by service; not by rhetoric, and above all not by insincere rhetoric, and that dreadful mental double-dealing and verbal juggling which makes promises and repudiates them, and says one thing at one time, and the directly opposite thing at another time. Our service must be the service of deeds.[13]

He went on to assert:

The most dangerous form of sentimental debauch is to give expression to good wishes on behalf of virtue while you do nothing about it. Justice is not merely words. It is to be translated into living acts.[14]

The infamous Margaret Sanger—who founded the vast Planned Parenthood network on such shocking pronouncements as, "The most *merciful* thing that a large family can do to one of its infant members is to *kill* it"[15] and "The marriage bed is the most *degenerating* influence in the social order"[16]—rightly saw Roosevelt as "a holdover from the old Christian religion," and thus a serious obstacle to her revolutionary program which called for "no Gods and no masters."[17]

Theodore Roosevelt stood foursquare on the legacy of Biblical orthodoxy and pro-life advocacy. He often asserted that he was "proud of his Holland, Huguenot, and Covenanting ancestors, and proud that the blood of that stark Puritan divine Jonathan Edwards flows in the veins" of his children.[18] For a time, he was able to sway public opinion. But as great a man as he was, he simply could not hold back the tide on his own. The dam had broken.

Progressivism

At the turn of the century, the urgent problems brought on by dramatic changes in the cultural and industrial landscape demanded immediate and innovative solutions. Progressivism offered such solutions. Under the dynamic leadership of Roosevelt in the U.S. and Hilaire Belloc in Europe, the movement produced a powerful groundswell of united support for sweeping social, political, and economic reforms. Rights were secured for organized labor; political machines were called into account; and massive commercial trusts were reined in.

Despite those remarkable successes, however, Progressivism was a short-lived movement. It quickly splintered into wildly divergent special interest factions. In America, once Roosevelt left his "bully pulpit" in the White House,

Henry Cabot Lodge and Charles Lindbergh, Sr. valiantly tried to carry on Progressivism's tradition—as informed by Christian conviction, patriotism, and family values. In Europe, once Belloc left his seat in the House of Commons, Cecil Chesterton and Maurice Baring likewise attempted to uphold Progressivism's legacy. In both cases, however, the bulk of the once mighty movement simply dissipated.

The fact is, among the movement's disparate factions and interests, there were a large number of irreverent and impatient young radicals who were informed by a very different ideological standard: the revolutionary philosophies and ideals of the humanistic enlightenment. They pushed the bulk of Progressivism into the fringes of Western politics and culture, establishing dozens of groups intent on the utter decimation of the Christian vision of life, liberty, and the pursuit of happiness: the Mugwumps, the Anarchists, the Knights of Labor, the Grangers, the Single-Taxers, the Suffragettes, the International Workers of the World, the Populists, and the Communists. But perhaps the most dangerous and influential off-shoots of Progressivism's new humanistic fragmentation was Malthusianism.

Thomas Malthus was a late eighteenth century professor of political economy whose mathematical theories convinced an entire generation of scientists, intellectuals, and social reformers that the world was facing an imminent economic crisis caused by unchecked human fertility. According to his scheme, population grows exponentially over time, while food production only grows arithmetically. Thus, poverty, deprivation, and hunger are simply evidences of a population problem. A responsible social policy will, therefore, address population growth as its most pressing priority. In fact, Malthus argued, to attempt to deal with endemic needs in any other way simply aggravates things all the further.

Malthus made the dystopic implications of his thinking crystal clear. In his definitive work, *An Essay on the Principle of Population,* first released in 1798, he wrote:

All children born, beyond what would be required to keep up the population to a desired level, must necessarily perish, unless room is made for them by the deaths of grown persons. Therefore we should facilitate, instead of foolishly and vainly endeavoring to impede, the operations of nature in producing this mortality; and if we dread the too frequent visitation of the horrid form of famine, we should sedulously encourage the other forms of destruction, which we compel nature to use. Instead of recommending cleanliness to the poor, we should encourage contrary habits. In our towns, we should make the streets narrower, crowd more people into the houses, and court the return of the plague. In the country, we should build our villages near stagnant pools, and particularly encourage settlement in all marshy and unwholesome situations. But above all, we should reprobate specific remedies for ravaging diseases; and restrain those benevolent, but much mistaken men, who have thought they were doing a service to mankind by projecting schemes for the total extirpation of particular disorders.[19]

The followers of Malthus believed that if Western civilization were to survive, the physically unfit, the materially poor, the spiritually diseased, the racially inferior, and the mentally incompetent had to be eliminated. The question was how? A few believed the solution to that dilemma was political—restrict immigration, centralize planning, reform social welfare, and tighten citizenship requirements. Some others thought the solution was technological—control agricultural production, regulate medical proficiency, and nationalize industrial efficiency. But the vast majority of Malthusians felt that the solution was genetic—restrict or remove "bad racial stocks," discourage charity and benevolence, and "aid the evolutionary ascent of man." Through selective breeding, eugenic repatterning, and craniometric specificity, they hoped to purify the bloodlines and improve the stock of the "highest" and "most fit"—or Aryan— race. Through segregation, sterilization, birth control, and abortion, they hoped to winnow the "lower" and "inferior" races out of the population—like chaff is from wheat.

These ideas found their way into some of the most significant political and social programs of the twentieth century.

Adolf Hitler adopted the ideas of Malthus in a wholesale fashion in his administration of the Third Reich—his exterminative "final solution," his coercive abortion program in Poland, Yugoslavia, and Czechoslovakia, and his elitist national socialism. He echoed the Malthusian call to "rid the earth of dysgenic peoples by whatever means available so that we may enjoy the prosperity of the Fatherland."[20] And he reiterated the Malthusian ideal of eliminating any Christian mercy ministries or social service programs. "Let us spend our efforts and our resources," he cried in a frenetic speech in 1939, "on the productive, not on the wastrel."[21]

Josef Stalin also wove the Malthusian ideal into his brutal interpretation of Marxism—his Ukrainian triage, his collectivization of the Kulaks, and his Siberian genocide. He argued that, "The greatest obstacle to the successful completion of the people's revolution is the swarming of inferior races from the south and east."[22] And the only thing that kept him from eliminating that obstacle was "the foolhardy interference of church charity."[23] That is why he made all Christian philanthropies illegal in 1929.

Similarly, in America, Margaret Sanger made Malthusian thinking the cornerstone of her endeavors—her attempts to smuggle contraband contraceptives into the country, her foiled campaign to send obscene materials through the mail, and her advocacy of promiscuous sex and abortion.[24] She was thoroughly convinced that the "inferior races" were in fact "human weeds" and a "menace to civilization."[25] She believed that "social regeneration" would only be possible as the "sinister forces of the hoards of irresponsibility and imbecility" were repulsed.[26] She accepted the Malthusian notion that organized Christian charity to ethnic minorities and the poor was a "symptom of a malignant social disease" because it encouraged the prolificacy of "defectives, delinquents, and dependents."[27]

Clearly, the practical import of Malthusianism— whether grafted into Nazism, Stalinism, or Planned Parenthood Eugenicism—was that abortion, infanticide, abandonment, and euthanasia were advocated as social *virtues* and that traditional Christian values were derided as *vices*. It was that killing was offered as a beneficent solution to a plethora of planetary crises of monumental proportions. For the first time since the time of Plato and Aristotle, a consistent pagan philosophy had been formulated to ethically defend genocide—and, for the first time it was systematically implemented. The Scripturally-rooted Progressivism of Roosevelt had been turned completely on its head.

Turning a Deaf Ear

When Balak, regent of the ancient kingdom of Moab, was confronted by the advancing armies of Israel immediately following the Exodus sojourn, he began to cast about for a strategy to defeat them (see Numbers 22:2–3). Military confrontation seemed hopeless. Diplomatic appeasement seemed suicidal. And defensive alliances seemed delinquent (see Numbers 22:4). So in desperation, he sent for Balaam, a conjurer and diviner, who was thought to have the power to bless and bind through spells and incantations (see Numbers 22:5–6).

Balak wanted to hire Balaam to curse Israel.

At first the magician was reluctant to take part in Balak's ploy, despite his generous offer (see Numbers 22:15–35). But eventually he gave in and delivered four oracles (see Numbers 22:36–24:25). Much to Balak's chagrin, however, each of the oracles predicted that Israel was invincible from without. No army, no king, no nation, and no empire would be able to stand against it. The only way God's chosen people could be defeated was if they defeated themselves from within—through disobedience and moral defilement.

That was all Balak needed to know. He didn't need an army. He didn't need diplomats. He didn't need allies. And now, he didn't even need diviners. All he needed was something to tempt Israel away from its fidelity.

He chose sex. He sent the most beautiful women in all of Moab down into Israel's camp at Peor (see Numbers 25:1–3, 6). Enticing the people to play the harlot, those women were able to do what no warrior or general ever could: tempt and trap Israel. And not a sword was drawn. Not an arrow was unsheathed. Not a javelin was hurled.

The people were dragged off into captivity by their own lust. They were defeated by the compromise of their Biblical standards.

The disintegration of Progressivism and the emergence of Malthusianism was more the sad consequence of the church's rueful recalcitrance than humanism's proud proficiency.

Under the influence of romantic and existential sentiment, believers absolutized the intuitions of individual conscience rather than the certainties of revealed external standards. Under the barrage of Darwinian and Malthusian prevarication, the bulk of the church began to confuse *the moral faculty*—the ability to make choices—with *the moral good*. Subjective whims and fashions were given the weight of objective authority and truth. The Balak temptation once again did its work.

In 1930, after an all-out lobbying effort by Margaret Sanger's staff, the Committee on Marriage and the Home of the Federal Council of Churches—a precursor to the National Council—became the first major organization in the history of Christendom to affirm the language and philosophy of "choice."[28] Soon after, the Quakers, the Northern Presbyterians, the Congregational church, the Methodist-Episcopal church, and several Baptist denominations followed suit. In Germany, the cooperating church gave tacit approval of Hitler's harsh *Erbgedsundheitsgetz* laws, which prescribed compulsory abortions, sterilizations, and eugenic controls for "dysgenic" peoples throughout occupied Eastern Europe—including the "final solution" that had been devised for the Jews. Finally, even the Lambeth conference of Anglican bishops capitulated to the Malthusian presuppositions.

When the Catholic church bemoaned this gross abdication of historic orthodoxy, several leading Protestants from around the world offered a defense arguing that God "is revealed in the endless sweep of evolution and His message is being slowly translated by science into the accents of the human tongue." Instead of relying on the Bible or Christian tradition, they said, the church should be guided by "the light of the evidence, the knowledge, and the experience of our time."[29]

It was not long before an avalanche of compromise occurred. One denomination after another turned a deaf ear on the unborn innocents and capitulated to the Balak temptation.

The United Church of Christ—which had led the prolife charge just two generations earlier—affirmed "the sacredness of all life, and the need to protect human life in particular," but then went on to uphold "the right of men and women to have access to adequately funded family planning services, and to safe and legal abortions as one option among others."[30]

The United Methodist church declared:

> Our belief in the sanctity of unborn human life makes us reluctant to approve abortion. But we are equally bound to respect the sacredness of life and well-being of the mother for whom devastating damage may result from an unacceptable pregnancy. In continuity with past Christian teaching, we recognize tragic conflicts of life with life that may justify abortion, and in such cases support the legal option of abortion under proper medical procedures.[31]

The Friends church asserted:

> On religious, moral, and humanitarian grounds, we arrived at the view that it is far better to end an unwanted pregnancy than to encourage the evils resulting from forced pregnancy and childbirth. We therefore urge the repeal of all laws limiting either the circumstances under which a woman may have an abortion or the physician's freedom to use his or her best professional judgment in performing it.[32]

The American Baptist churches baptized the Malthusian rhetoric saying:

> We grieve with all who struggle with the difficult circumstances that lead them to consider abortion. Recognizing that each person is ultimately responsible to God, we encourage women and men in these circumstances to seek spiritual counsel as they prayerfully and conscientiously consider abortion.[33]

The largest Lutheran communions worldwide reaffirmed the principles of their Nazi collaboration by stating:

> In the consideration of induced abortion, the key issue is the status of the unborn fetus. Since the fetus is the organic beginning of human life, the termination of its development is always a serious matter. Nevertheless, a qualitative distinction must be made between its claims and the rights of a responsible person made in God's image who is living in relationships with God and other human beings. This understanding of responsible personhood is congruent with the historical Lutheran teaching and practice whereby only living persons are baptized. On the basis of the evangelical ethic, a woman or couple may decide responsibly to seek an abortion.[34]

Even a large number of prominent evangelical leaders yielded to the Balak temptation. Meeting under the auspices of *Christianity Today* magazine and the Christian Medical Society, and led by the highly esteemed Carl F. H. Henry, the evangelicals engaged in debate and exchanged papers for several days before they drafted a consensus report. Published later in the magazine, the report said in part:

> Changes in the state laws on therapeutic abortion should be encouraged.
>
> Suitable cases for abortion would fall within the scope of the American College of Obstetricians and Gynecologists Statement on Abortion.
>
> As to whether or not the performance of an induced abortion is always sinful we are not agreed, but about the permissibility for it under certain circumstances we are in accord.
>
> The Christian physician will advise induced abortion only to safeguard greater values sanctioned by Scripture. These values should include individual health, family welfare, and social responsibility.
>
> Much human suffering can be alleviated by preventing the birth of children where there is a predictable high risk of genetic disease or abnormality. This appears to be a reasonable Christian objective.[35]

With the massive defection of so much of the church from its historic role as the defender of the innocents, the pro-abortion forces were able to easily roll back legal impediments to child-killing:

- In 1925, abortion is legalized in the Soviet Union.

- In 1931, Hitler also legalizes abortion and launches his eugenics plan for Germany and Eastern Europe.

- In 1938, Sweden becomes the first free nation in Christendom to revert to pre-Christian abortion legislation.

- Between 1949 and 1956, abortion is legalized in eleven other European nations.

- In 1954, Planned Parenthood holds an international conference on abortion and calls for "reform" of restrictive legislation.

- In 1962, the American Law Institute proposes that abortion laws be decriminalized.

- In 1966, the National Organization of Women is established with the liberalization of abortion laws as a major goal.

- In 1967, the American Medical Association reverses its century old commitment to the lives of the unborn and also begins calling for decriminalization of abortion.

- During that same year, three states—Colorado, California, and North Carolina—loosen restrictions on certain child-killing procedures.

- In 1968, the United Kingdom legalizes abortion.

- In 1970, four more states—Hawaii, Alaska, Washington, and New York—enact abortion-on-demand legislation.

- By the end of 1971, nearly half a million legal abortions are being performed in the U.S. each year.

- Then in 1973, the Supreme Court issues its momentous *Roe v. Wade* decree that changes the abortion laws in all fifty states by sheer judicial fiat.

It seemed that the lone Christian voice of dissent during this tidal wave of neo-pagan revivalism was the Catholic church. On July 29, 1968, Pope Paul VI issued his *Humanae Vitae* encyclical which, among other things, reaffirmed the church's commitment to the sanctity of life. Thus, it appeared that only the Catholic church remained uncompromisingly pro-life—and as a result, the abortion issue came to be viewed in the public arena as "a Catholic issue."

Standing Against the Tide

Actually, there were any number of believers who remained steadfast in their commitment to life—Protestant, Eastern Orthodox, as well as Catholic. In the face of the crushing twentieth century abortion juggernaut—that moved from Malthusianism to Nazism to Stalinism to Planned Parenthood eugenicism to government sanctioned child-killing in decisions like *Roe v. Wade*—there was an unwavering rem-

nant that maintained the church's long-held witness for justice, truth, and life. Their vigil was often lonely and thank-
less—but it was sure:

- *G. K. Chesterton* was one of the brightest minds of his
  age—a prolific journalist, best-selling novelist, popular
  debater, and profound humorist. He was also one of
  the most faithful defenders of life against the on-
  slaughts of neo-pagan modernism. The great Christian
  apologist fired unrelenting salvos of biting analysis
  against the Malthusians, indicting them for "combining
  a hardening of the heart with a sympathetic softening
  of the head,"[36] and for presuming to turn "common
  decency" and "commendable deeds" into "social
  crimes."[37] If Darwinism was the doctrine of "the survival of the fittest," then he said, Malthusianism was the
  doctrine of "the survival of the nastiest."[38] In his remarkably visionary book, *Eugenics and Other Evils,* he
  ably pointed out—for the first time anywhere—the link
  between Malthusian Eugenics and the evolution of
  Prussian and Volkish Monism into Fascist Nazism. "It is
  the same stuffy science," he argued, "the same bullying
  bureaucracy, and the same terrorism by tenth-rate professors, that has led the German Empire to its recent
  conspicuous triumphs."[39]

- *Pope Pius XI* understood the implications of the National Socialist Party's Malthusian theory and condemned it throughout the final decade of his life. He
  referred to Hitler's fascist philosophy as a "paganism of
  state," and declared "We are living in times when racial
  pride has been exalted to the point of being a pride of
  thoughts, doctrines, and practices, which is neither
  Christian nor human."[40] His pro-life encyclical *Mit
  Brennender Sorge* condemned Nazism, saying: "The cul-
  minating point of Revelation reached in the gospel of
  Jesus Christ is definitive; it is forever binding. This Revelation knows no extension added by the hand of man;
  it does not allow itself to be supplanted and replaced
  by arbitrary revelations which certain spokesmen of the

present time claim to derive from what they call the myth of blood and race."[41] This encyclical was secretly distributed and read in all the Catholic churches of the Reich. After Pius's death in 1939, the Grand Rabbi of Rome actually converted to the Christian faith—because of his friend's clear and unmitigated testimony in word and in deed.

- *Cardinal Pacelli* succeeded Pius XI as Pope Pius XII and continued Catholic opposition to "the neo-pagan doctrines" of the Nazis. In his first encyclical, *Summi Pontificatus,* he condemned "exacerbated nationalism, the idolatry of the state, totalitarianism, racism, the cult of brutal force, contempt of international agreements," and, in short, "all the characteristics of Hitler's political system."[42] When Jews were rounded up in France and deported to Germany in 1942, the collaborating governments tried to get at least partial support from the Vatican but were severely rebuffed. Pius XII twice agreed to directly contact the highest level of the German civil and military Resistance in order to represent it before the London War Cabinet. Though events led to the cancellation of the plan, the Pope led many in the church, both Catholic and Protestant to reject Nazi ideology as anti-Christian paganism and actively resist and rescue. More than once he publicly brought attention to "the anxious supplications of all those who, because of their nationality or their race, are overwhelmed by the greatest trials and most acute distress, and at times even destined, without any personal fault, to measures of extermination."[43]

- In 1936, *Bishop Clemens Count von Galen* of Münster delivered a devastating sermon condemning the Nazi extermination of handicapped adults deemed "unfit" by Hitler's "race hygiene" program. He articulated the historic orthodox position that the Christians must protect the innocent even at the risk of their own lives: "It is said of these patients: They are like an old machine which no longer runs, like an old horse which is hopelessly paralyzed, like a cow which no longer gives milk.

But these are horridly false metaphors. We are not talking here about a machine, a horse, nor a cow. No, we
are talking about men and women, our compatriots,
our brothers and sisters. Poor unproductive people if
you wish, but does this mean that they have lost their
right to live?"[44] He prophesied God's wrath on those
"sending innocent people to their death."[45] And he
spoke for the Christian community asserting, "We wish
to withdraw ourselves and our faithful from their influence, so that we may not be contaminated by their
thinking and their ungodly behavior, so that we may
not participate and share with them in the punishment
which a just God should and will pronounce upon all
those who—like ungrateful Jerusalem—do not wish
what God wishes."[46] Galen's sermon was widely distributed throughout Germany and proved to be one of the
primary catalysts for the underground resistance in
both the occupied regions and in Germany itself.

- *Corrie ten Boom* lived with her father and sister in
Haarlam, Holland where she assisted in the family
watchmaking business and ministered to a number of
mentally retarded children. Early in 1940, the nation
fell to the invading Germans. Though at first the occu-
pation seemed bearable enough to Corrie and her family, gradually her Christian conscience was pained as
she saw more and more evidence of anti-Semitic persecution. When Jews began to disappear, together the ten
Booms began plotting ways to subvert the Nazi's murderous designs. Eventually, their home became the hub
of the Dutch underground in Haarlam. A secret room
was put in one of the bedrooms so that they could hide
Jews. In 1944, Corrie was arrested—along with her sister and her father who both eventually died in German
concentration camps—for their illicit pro-life rescue efforts. Providentially, Corrie was released from prison
just a week before her cell block was to be extermi-
nated. For the rest of her life, Corrie traveled around
the world sharing the consolation and the power of life
in Christ.

- Born into the privilege of a prominent upper-class German family, *Dietrich Bonhoeffer* studied theology at the
University of Tübingen—the seedbed of Continental
liberalism—and received his doctorate from the University of Berlin. Beginning in 1933, Bonhoeffer risked
his scholarly life of ease by openly criticizing the policies of the Third Reich. He was active in opposing Hitler, not only because of the Nazi eugenic programs, but
because of the regime's active promotion of abortion.
"Destruction of the embryo in the mother's womb," he
charged, "is a violation of the right to live which God
has bestowed upon this nascent life." After serving as a
pastor to the exile community in London for two years,
he returned to Germany in 1935 to teach at an unau-
thorized "alternative" seminary. Two years later the
school was shut down by the Gestapo. Bonhoeffer was
banned from preaching and teaching and was thus
forced to continue his discipling and pro-life ministries
covertly. In 1944, he was implicated in a conspiracy that
had been linked to the German resistance and was sent
to the gallows for treason the following year—just days
before the Allied liberation.

- Beginning in 1934, *Vladimir Saravov* served as a deacon
in a small parish church on the banks of the Dnieper
River near the great city of Kiev. Although his duties
were primarily liturgical, he was also responsible for
channeling his congregation's covert aid to families
fleeing Stalin's persecution of Ukrainian Kulaks. As he
supplied food, clothing, medicines, and shelter to these
refugees, he was startled to discover that not only were
they victims of socialization, collectivization, and soviet-
ization, many had been coerced to undergo abortion
and sterilization procedures. Outraged, Vladimir organized underground resistance to the Red Army doctors
in order to rescue both the children and their mothers—by diverting supply lines, hiding refugees, and providing alternative medical care. Though he was martyred for his activities in 1939, several fellow deacons

continued his work throughout the tumultuous Stalin years.

- *Lars Tanner* was raised in a large working-class Norwegian Lutheran home in Oslo. When he was a teenager, his family moved to Stockholm where he lived and worked as a cobbler for the rest of his life. A series of devastating miscarriages suffered by his wife provoked him to delve into the Bible's teaching about children. Startled by what he discovered, he began to wonder why the church had not taken a stronger stand the previous year when many restrictions on abortion were lifted. Beginning with a small newsletter printed on a crude press in his cellar, he dedicated himself to an educational campaign that would eventually span nearly four decades—testifying before hospital committees and government hearings, lecturing to secondary and university students, lobbying candidates for political office, and organizing protests at abortuary sites. By the time of his death in 1975, he had laid the groundwork for a resurgent pro-life movement in Sweden and had set an example of faithfulness for thousands of Christians throughout Scandinavia.

- Born in Northern Ireland to a wealthy Presbyterian family, *Amy Beatrice Carmichael* became one of the best known missionaries of the first half of the twentieth century. Her ministry took her first to Japan, then to Ceylon, and finally to the Dohnavur province of India. Although *sarti* and *immolation* had been legally banned, to her horror she discovered that ritual abortion and female infanticide were still quite common. In addition, many of the young girls that she had come to work with were still being systematically sold off as slaves to the nearby pagan temples in order to be raised as cult prostitutes. She immediately established a ministry to protect and shelter the girls. Although she had to suffer the persecution of various Hindu sects and the bureaucratic resistance of the British colonial government, Carmichael built an effective and dynamic ministry renowned for its courage and compassion.

Sadly, many of her fellow missionaries in India—having partially accepted the presuppositions of Malthusian thought—believed that her effort to build an orphanage and school was actually a "worldly activity" that distracted her from the "saving of souls." To such accusations she simply replied, "Souls are more or less firmly attached to bodies."[47] Since her death in 1951, her Dohnavur Fellowship has continued to carry on ministries of evangelism, education, and medical aid among the poor and helpless.

- Birmingham, Alabama, was a wild and untamed mining town in the heart of the reconstructed South when *James Alexander Bryan* came to pastor the Third Presbyterian Church there in 1888. When he died in 1941, Birmingham had become a vibrant industrial center. In the years between, Brother Bryan—as he was affectionately called—won the hearts of generation after generation of citizens with his selfless service to the poor, the needy, the brokenhearted, and the sick. Known for his life of prayer and his indefatigable efforts to encourage the distressed, he was a faithful pro-life stalwart as well. When a Planned Parenthood representative came to Birmingham in 1937, he was a vocal critic, calling on Christians to uphold their legacy of concern and care. Shortly before his death, the city erected a statue of the pastor in a posture of prayer—a common sight—and proclaimed him "the patron saint of Birmingham."[48]

There were scores of other faithful Christians who stood for life during the West's mad rush toward modernity. They included Bertilla Boscardin (d. 1922), Charbel Makhlouf (d. 1898), Nectarius Kephalas (d. 1920), Maximilian Kolbe (d. 1941), Hans and Sophie Scholl (d. 1943), Henri de Lubac (d. 1987), Henry Cabot Lodge (d. 1924), Hilaire Belloc (d. 1953), Pope Paul VI (d. 1978), and Franciszek Blachnicki (d. 1987). Despite the recalcitrance of so much of the church, there was a remnant that had not yet bowed the knee to Baal. The legacy of hope continued uninterrupted despite the darkness of the days.

Conclusion

Historian and social commentator Milan Hubl has pointedly and bitingly argued that:

> The first step in liquidating a people is to erase its memory. Destroy its books, its culture, and its history; before long the community will forget what it is, and what it was.[49]

It seems that during much of the twentieth century, the memory of the church was erased. Its books, its culture, and its history were all but destroyed in the mad rush toward modernity. The community of faith forgot what it was and what it should have been. The result was that, despite the heroic efforts of a remnant of dissenters, the needy, the innocent, and the helpless lost their one sure advocate.

Predictably, this failure of Christian efficacy was rooted in the denial of five essential principles:

Orthodoxy

When believers began to abandon orthodoxy in a wholesale fashion, they simply exchanged the Christian system of moral standards that had brought Western culture to full flower for ancient pagan values. When the ethical system of the Bible is jettisoned, men are left to their own devices and thus quickly revert to destructive primal passions. There is no other alternative. There is no third way. There is no middle ground (see Matthew 12:30). Thus, when the church at the beginning of the twentieth century began to do "what was right in its own eyes" (Judges 21:25), chaos reigned and the innocent suffered.

The Church

Disunity racked the church during much of the twentieth century, not just an institutional and a denominational disunity, but a fundamental disunity of focus and purpose. Working at cross purposes with itself, the church tragically nullified its import and impact at the very time it was most needed. It abdicated its role as the pacesetter of art, music, and ideas, yielding to a new cultural and scientific high priesthood. A rapid slide into neo-paganism resulted, evidenced by the ascendency and acceptance of Hitler, Stalin, and Sanger.

Servanthood

A disinterested church inevitably becomes a self-serving church. After a flurry of evangelistic efforts around the world in the nineteenth century, missionary activity dropped precipitously in the twentieth. Relief and development projects, works of mercy, the establishment of hospitals, church planting, and outreaches to the needy ceased to be priorities. The unborn, the infirm, the unwanted, and the undesired simply could not compete with the jangling primacy for personal peace and affluence.

Urgency

Righteous indignation and holy zeal became all but endangered species during much of the century. Passions were turned inward, as were devotions. Virtues became vices, and the most awful of indulgences became canonized orthodoxies. Risk, jeopardy, and self-sacrifice were replaced by security, certainty, and self-gratification. Thus, the only urgency that drove much of the church during this dark period in history was its own satisfaction.

Patience

It was not assurance in the promises of God that stirred and motivated the bulk of the church in the twentieth century as much as it was the promises of science or experience. As a result, the attribute of patience virtually disappeared from Christendom; liberals opted for revolutionary tactics, and conservatives resorted to personal existential manifestations of faith. An easy "instant-everything" mentality developed so that believers would not have to face up to their responsibilities or live with the consequences of their actions. Thus, abortion became one of many expedients to dispatch unpleasant difficulties.

❧   ❧   ❧

There were, of course, exceptions to the ruling principles of the day—the whole of the Catholic church for one. In the face of the most awful tyrannies, pro-life stalwarts abounded. Still, it was a difficult time of stunning setbacks. It was a time that brought to mind Edgar Allan Poe's vivid vision in the story, "The Red Masque of Death":

> There were much glare and glitter and piquancy and phantasm. There were delirious fancies as the madman fashions. There were much of the beautiful, much of the wanton, much of the bizarre, something of the terrible, and not a little of that which might have excited disgust.[50]

RESCUE THE PERISHING: THE NEW PRO-LIFE EMERGENCE

dum vita est spes est [1]

A man who knows that the earth is round but lives among men who believe it to be flat ought to hammer in his doctrine of the earth's roundness up to the point of arrest, imprisonment, or even death. Reality will confirm him, and he is not so much testifying to the world as it is—which is worth nothing—as to Him who made the world, and Who is worth more than all things.

Hilaire Belloc

You cannot escape the revelation of the identical by taking refuge in the illusion of the multiple.

G. K. Chesterton

hough the story of the pro-life movement is a story of courage, conviction, and compassion, it is also the story of commonness. For twenty centuries it has been composed primarily of ordinary people. People with jobs and families. People with hopes and dreams. People with virtues and vices. Just common ordinary people. People like Barry and Marsha Leddler.

The Leddlers have been quietly demonstrating their commitment to the sanctity of human life over the past decade in a number of different ways. They are compulsive "joiners," Barry says, and thus, they are "members of virtually every pro-life organization under the sun—Christian Action Council, National Right to Life, American Life League, Black Americans for Life, Americans United for Life, Operation Rescue, LifeNet, and the Pro-Life Action League." Marsha serves as a volunteer counselor at a crisis pregnancy center for teens near a local high school. Barry leads a community coalition of men who provide pro-life news and information to local legislators, hospital administrators, and business leaders. And together, each Saturday morning, they do sidewalk counseling outside a particularly notorious Planned Parenthood abortion chamber.

Barry teaches sixth-grade boys in the Sunday school at a local Presbyterian church and is an assistant soccer coach in the Pee-Wee League. Marsha is a room mother for the second grade at their small community Christian school and coordinates the carpooling for a private ballet and gymnastics program run by several interested mothers. They enjoy backyard family barbecues and weekend hikes in the woods with their four elementary age children.

"Like most Christians we know," Barry says, "we were pretty uninvolved with things outside our private little circle for a long, long while. But as we began to grow in the faith—influenced particularly by the books of Francis Schaeffer—we realized that we had to apply our faith to every area of life. We realized that we had a responsibility to act on the basis of the Word."

Some time ago, they decided to uphold that responsibility to act by participating in a large protest organized by several cooperating pro-life groups. They had no idea how momentous that decision would be.

"The way the media talked about it later, you would have thought that some Libyan terrorists had sealed off half of Pittsburgh," Marsha said. "Actually, it was more like a really beautiful prayer meeting—with Bible reading, hymn singing, and quiet devoted prayer. No shouting. No shoving. There is no way that anyone could *honestly* call what we did out there *violent harassment* or anything even *close* to that—but then *honesty* is not exactly the media's strong suit these days."

Apparently, the police were concerned that the protest might indeed turn violent. So, with brutal efficiency they arrested more than one hundred of the peaceful men and women praying on the sidewalk and in the parking lot—including Barry and Marsha. "The men were transported to the North Side Police Station where we were forced to go without food for over thirty-three hours," Barry said. "A couple of diabetic and hypoglycemic men had to be rushed to a hospital emergency room for treatment of food deprivation."

"The women went to the North Side Station at first, but were then moved to the Allegheny County Jail," Marsha said. "It was awful. The prison guards were unbelievably rough. Several of us were grabbed by the fronts of our blouses and bras. Some even had their breasts totally exposed and fondled in full view of the other prisoners."

The next day, a number of the protesters were moved again, at the behest of the attorneys advising city and county officials—this time to the Mayview Psychiatric Hospital. "I couldn't believe it," Barry related. "They actually held us in the psych ward for nearly two days. They don't even do that sort of thing in Russia anymore."

The Leddlers filed an official complaint. And the district attorney has promised to launch an investigation.

These days, such investigations leave no good stone unturned. But then, they leave no good turn unstoned either.

Whatever Happened to Evangelicals?

In the years leading up to the *Roe v. Wade* decision, most Christians—like the Leddlers—were totally unaware of the abortion issue. When so many evangelical Christian leaders around the world—in lock-step with theological liberals—were guiding their congregations, seminaries, colleges, and denominations toward complete capitulation on the sanctity of life, most of the people in the pews were entirely incognizant of the terms of the debate. They didn't even know there *was* a debate.

For almost a full century, the greatest proportion of the evangelical community had been in a deep cultural hibernation. Thus, despite the largest, most powerful, richest, best organized, and most visible Christian consensus ever, the immoral and unstable humanistic juggernaut was able to gain full control of the cultural apparatus.

For several generations, evangelicals had deliberately and self-consciously abandoned the world. For all intents and purposes, they abandoned the Biblical and historic mandate to be salt and light (see Matthew 5:13–16). They even abandoned the practical dimensions of the Great Commission to nurture, disciple, and convert the nations (see Matthew 28:18–20). Instead, they emphasized a view of spirituality rooted—ironically enough—in pagan Greek thought.

This kind of religious Platonism, or pietism as it is often called, drew a sharp line of distinction between things that are *spiritual* and things that are *material*. Believing that the spiritual realm was vastly superior to the physical realm, pietism tended to spurn all things physical, all things temporal, and all things earthly. Art, music, and ideas were ignored—except perhaps for their value as propaganda. Activities that did not easily and immediately contribute to inner piety were neglected. The intellect was held suspect. And the pleasures of the flesh—regardless of how innocent or sacred—were condemned outright.

According to the dogmas of pietism, a Christian's efforts should be almost exclusively directed toward individualistic and quietistic devotion. Bible study, prayer, church attendance, and evangelism were to comprise the universe of tasks for the believer. Anything and everything else was thought to be a distraction and worldly. In short, Christians were to become, as the old aphorism says, "so heavenly minded that they are no earthly good."

And they did.

But meanwhile, back at the ranch, things were not going too terribly well. A sense of national malaise was spawned by endemic poverty, rampant crime, despoiling drugs, proliferating pornography, blatant racism, epidemic divorce, uncontrollable plagues, widespread illiteracy, burgeoning homelessness, impotent foreign policy, and declining economic prowess. Beginning in the mid-seventies, evangelicals awoke from their fever dream jolted by the sudden realization that their whole world was falling apart. The liberties that had facilitated their prior irrelevance were now very much in jeopardy.

Evangelical leaders began to call on Christians to stand in the public arena and apply the principles of the gospel to every aspect of their lives—both in the inner realm of piety and in the outer realm of polity. In 1978, Jerry Falwell's Moral Majority was organized. Shortly afterward, James Dobson's Focus on the Family, Pat Robertson's Freedom Council, John Whitehead's Rutherford Institute, Beverly LaHaye's Concerned Women for America, and D. James Kennedy's President's Council joined veteran groups like Howard Phillip's Conservative Caucus, Phyllis Schlafly's Eagle Forum, Paul Weyrich's Free Congress Foundation, and Rus Walton's Plymouth Rock Foundation on the front lines. Soon these organizations were working in tandem in order to mobilize Christians like Barry and Marsha Leddler on the crucial issues of the day.

At least to some degree, they succeeded. The phenomenon of the "Christian Right" became an essential element of the American political and cultural landscape. And, though victories seemed to be few and far between, much of the church was at long last intimately involved in the affairs of God's world once again.

Reinventing the Wheel

As evangelicals began to rediscover their Biblical responsibilities in the world, the issue of abortion emerged as their premier concern. For many who had been honest enough to genuinely investigate it, abortion was no longer merely a matter of theological or legal debate. It was the horrifying and brutal destruction of human life—children ripped limb from limb or burned to death by toxic solutions or crushed and vacuumed out of the womb.

For them, abortion ceased to be an *issue.* An *issue* is, after all, something that we can reasonably and rationally discuss around a negotiating table. An *issue* is something that we can compromise on. It is something that involves give and take. It is something that we can ponder, argue, and debate. Indeed, it is something that good men and women can legitimately disagree on. We can juggle its niggling little points back and forth. Or we can do nothing at all. We can take it or leave it.

As they became more and better informed, Christians realized that abortion is none of those things. Instead, it is a matter of life and death. It is a test of faith. It is perhaps the *ultimate* test of faith in these difficult and complex times. And thus, they discovered, it demands uncompromising, unwavering, and unhesitating faithful action.

It was not long before a number of influential voices began calling on all Christians—Protestant and Orthodox, as well as Catholic—to answer that call to action:

- In 1973, shortly after the *Roe v. Wade* decision, James McFaddon, a longtime *National Review* staffer, launches the Ad Hoc Committee in the Defense of Life on Capitol Hill.

- In 1975, a number of evangelical leaders meet in the home of Billy Graham for two days in order to formulate a Scriptural response to the crisis at hand. The result of the meeting is the formation of a new pro-life education and advocacy organization—the Christian Action Council.

- In 1978, the American Life League is formed to parallel—and extend the limits of—the work of the National Right to Life Committee.

- In 1979, Francis Schaeffer releases his remarkable book and film series *Whatever Happened to the Human Race?*, but is met at first with a stony silence. Even so, the slumbering conscience begins to awaken in evangelicalism.

- A year later, *Moody Monthly,* a Christian family magazine issues a clarion call to evangelical action: "Evangelicalism as a whole has uttered no real outcry. We've organized no protest. Do we need time to think abortion through? Isn't seven years enough? The Catholics have called abortion *the Silent Holocaust.* The deeper horror is the silence of the Evangelical."[2] Within months the silence begins to shatter.

- Shortly thereafter, in 1981, Schaeffer releases another ground-breaking book, *A Christian Manifesto,* which begins to galvanize the nascent pro-life forces.

- In 1985, the film *The Silent Scream,* hosted by former abortion rights leader Bernard Nathanson, shatters the illusion that the procedure is anything less than child-killing—and thus thrusts the debate onto the national stage.

Despite these landmark events, it seemed for a time that evangelical indifference would continue indefinitely. But suddenly, an avalanche of concern transformed the church. By 1985, twenty-eight Protestant denominations, associations, and missions had recanted their earlier pro-abortion positions including the single largest evangelical denomination—and arguably the most influential—the Southern Baptist Convention.

Before the end of the decade, virtually every evangelical leader in America had publicly committed himself in some way to upholding the sanctity of life in both word and deed. As Chuck Swindoll confessed, "Remaining silent is no longer an option."[3]

Armed with this new sense of accord, and with apparently committed pro-life Presidents in the White House for over a decade, most Christians seemed certain that the abortion consensus would at last be rolled back. Sadly, a series of events would seriously minimize the impact of the pro-life forces:

- In 1978, serious infighting erupts between the veteran groups and the various upstarts. Ideological, methodological, and theological differences explode into full-scale animosity.

- In 1980, new conflicts arise between Catholic and Protestant groups.

- In 1982, advocacy of two conflicting pro-life bills on Capitol Hill—the Hatch and the Helms measures—cripples any hope of congressional action and exposes both the disarray and the naiveté of the movement.

- In 1984, a spate of abortion clinic bombings rocks the pro-life community.

- In 1987, Planned Parenthood launches a full-scale negative publications campaign to discredit and close the more than three thousand alternative crisis pregnancy centers around the country.

- Rescue missions, beginning in New York and Atlanta in 1988, sweep across the country reinvigorating many, but once again deeply dividing movement forces and drawing the ire of recalcitrant church leaders.

- In 1989, sit-ins and rescue operations began to face serious attrition due to the severe treatment of police and the heavy penalties exacted by prosecutors.

- That same year, after the Supreme Court essentially disables *Roe* by returning regulatory powers to states in the Missouri *Webster* case, pro-life forces are demoralized by the defection of a number of politicians and by innumerable legislative obstacles.

Despite these setbacks, a number of successes kept weary believers from surrendering to despair:

- In 1989, the *Webster* decision not only puts abortion back in the public arena, but it also allows legislatures to draft restrictive legislation.

- In 1990, National Right to Life hosts a rally at the Washington Monument that not only attracts more than five hundred thousand participants and clarifies the problem of anti-Christian bigotry in the national news media, but it also galvanizes and encourages believers to carry on with the struggle come what may.

- Later that same year, American Life League successfully conducts a satellite broadcast rally designed to unify all the various factions and organizations in the movement.

Throughout its entire rollercoaster ride since *Roe,* the pro-life movement has continued to attempt to carve out a niche for itself in the centuries-old legacy of faithfulness.

Seizing the Day

The theology of deliverance runs all throughout the Bible. Again and again, Scripture exhorts the faithful to rescue the weak, in one way or another, out of the strong jaws of death.

God Himself is the great rescuer:

In that day there will be an altar to the LORD in the
midst of the land of Egypt, and a pillar to the LORD near
its border. And it will become a sign and a witness to the
LORD of hosts in the land of Egypt; for they will cry to
the LORD because of oppressors, and He will send them
a Savior and a Champion, and He will rescue them.
(Isaiah 19:19–20)

He rescues the humble (Psalm 76:9). He rescues the
afflicted (see Psalm 35:10). And He rescues the ravaged
(see Psalm 35:17). He rescues each of His own from the
wicked (see Psalm 17:13), from the deceitful and dishonest
(see Psalm 43:1), from temptation (see 2 Peter 2:9), from
every evil deed (see 2 Timothy 4:18), from our bodies of
sin and death (see Romans 7:24–25), and from this present
age (see Galatians 1:4).

As His disciples, we are to comfort others with the very
comfort we ourselves have received (see 2 Corinthians 1:4).
Thus, we too are to be deliverers:

Thus says the LORD: "Do justice and righteousness, and
rescue those who have been robbed by the power of the
oppressor." (Jeremiah 22:3a)

Vindicate the weak and fatherless; Do justice to the afflicted and destitute. Rescue the weak and needy; Deliver
them out of the hand of the wicked. (Psalm 82:3–4, NKJV)

Rescue those who are being dragged away to death, and
those who are staggering to the slaughter, O hold them
back. If you say, "See we did not know this," does He not
consider it who weighs the hearts? And does He not
know it who keeps your soul? And will He not render to
a man according to his work? (Proverbs 24:11–12, NKJV)

There are those, who even amidst the confusion of the
present day—with all its fickle political profundities—have
heard that high call to covenantal faithfulness. Their stories
are a testament to the grace of the Deliverer—who in turn
calls us to deliver. In a rapturous variety of manners, methods, and means, they have heard and heeded that call:

- In 1910, *Agnes Gonxha Bojaxhiu* was born in Skopje, near what is today the Albanian-Yugoslav border. After receiving a Christian education, she joined the Sisters of Loretto, an Irish order of missionary nuns working in India. Taking the name Teresa, she taught in a convent school for upper-class Indian girls for two decades before founding a slum school in 1948. Two years later, she began the Order of the Missionaries of Charity, which was dedicated to serving the poor. Providing food, medical care, and shelter to destitute lepers, homeless children, and the poorest of the poor, Teresa's order has grown into a worldwide movement of over eighteen hundred sisters in nearly two hundred branches. In 1979, she was awarded the Nobel Peace Prize. To the dismay of many, she used the opportunity to express her horror at the revival of abortion practices even within Christendom. In the days that followed, her pro-life pronouncements became both more frequent and more strident. Even after her retirement from active ministry in 1990, *Mother Teresa* has maintained a high profile wherever and whenever the defenseless are threatened.

- Variously called the "Guru of the Fundamentalists," "Missionary to the Intellectuals," and "Godfather of Evangelicalism," *Francis A. Schaeffer* was undoubtedly one of the most influential thinkers, theologians, authors, and apologists of the past generation. After serving for a short time in Presbyterian congregations in the United States, he moved to Switzerland in 1948 to begin a unique missionary outreach, to whoever God would send to his door. Over the years, literally thousands of students, skeptics, and searchers found their way to the door of the small mountain chalet that he shared with his wife and four children. Calling his work L'Abri—the French word for shelter—he set up a study center and simply attempted to provide "honest answers to honest questions." Asserting the lordship of Christ over the totality of life, he wrote a series of intellectually stimulating books documenting the drift of

Western art, music, ideas, and law from their Christian moorings. Though he had a wide following among academically minded evangelicals beginning in the mid-sixties, it was not until the 1979 release of his book and film series, *Whatever Happened to the Human Race,* that he gained national and international notoriety. Despite a difficult and protracted battle against cancer, over the next five years, he gave the lion's share of his time, energies, and efforts to the pro-life cause. In both word and deed, Schaeffer confirmed the gospel's message of light and life.

- As a Christian physician, *Jack C. Willke* recognized the importance of offering honest dialogue and information to young people about their sexuality, if they were to make responsible and ethical decisions. Writing with his wife, Barbara, he published his first book on the subject in 1964. By the early seventies, the Willkes were regularly being asked to give their presentation, including a discussion on the dangers of abortion, to Bible study meetings, youth groups, and campus assemblies. After the *Roe v. Wade* decision, Dr. Willke began a long tenure of service on the board of the National Right to Life Committee. In 1980, he became the president of that prestigious education and advocacy organization, leading it through a tumultuous decade of expansion. Early in 1990, he organized the largest rally in the history of the nation's capital, with more than half a million Christians taking their stand for life.

- For more than ten years before the fateful *Roe v. Wade* decision, *Paul Marx* had been preaching against the horrors of child-killing. In 1971, he attended a national seminar for medical professionals entitled "Therapeutic Abortion: A Symposium on Implementation." Afterward, he wrote the blockbuster exposé, *The Death Peddlers: War on the Unborn.* He followed that with another stunning piece of detective work in the crusade to legitimate euthanasia, *The Mercy Killers.* In 1972, he established the Human Life Center at St. John's University, which later moved to the University of Steubenville. In

1981, he founded Human Life International—the foremost multi-national pro-life organization today. With chapters in twenty-two nations in every corner of the world and work in dozens more, Father Marx has literally become a pro-life missionary to the world.

- Every year since 1977, *Phyllis Schlafly* has been named as one of the ten most admired women in the world by the readers of *Good Housekeeping* magazine. And little wonder. A renowned Harvard-educated attorney, nationally syndicated columnist, radio commentator, bestselling author, devoted wife, mother of six children, and president of the conservative pro-family organization, Eagle Forum, Mrs. Schlafly has been generally credited with single-handedly organizing the grassroots forces that foiled the ratification of the feminist inspired Equal Rights Amendment to the U.S. Constitution. In addition, she has been unflagging in her efforts on behalf of the unborn—testifying before more than fifty Congressional and state legislative committees and catalyzing an army of housewives, mothers, and grandmothers all over the country.

- *Joan Andrews* was sentenced to five years in prison in 1986 for the crime of attempting to save children from certain death at a Florida abortion clinic. In the case immediately preceding hers, two men who were convicted of murder were sentenced to four years apiece. As word of this judicial travesty slowly made its way out into the pro-life community, Joan's sacrifice became a paramount symbol of Christian commitment and compassion. Involved in all aspects of the pro-life movement—protests, sidewalk counseling, crisis sheltering, and non-violent rescues—since the early seventies, she was soon devoting herself to the defense of the unborn as a full-time ministry. Today her efforts span the globe, having rescued throughout both Western and Eastern Europe.

- Creating a storm of controversy wherever he goes, *Randall Terry* is one of the most dynamic leaders in a new generation of pro-life activists and strategists. As the founder of Operation Rescue, he helped spark a whole new level of interest, concern, debate, and confrontation over abortion. In 1984, he opened a small clinic offering alternatives to women caught in the midst of crisis pregnancies. By 1986, he began conducting sit-ins at abortion clinics in an attempt to close the facilities and prevent killing procedures from taking place. In May 1988, massive protests in New York and Atlanta focused national attention on Terry—who was still in his twenties—and his fledgling movement. Over the next two years Operation Rescue mobilized thousands upon thousands of Christians to place their bodies between the abortionists and the children. Over fifty thousand arrests resulted—more than five times as many arrests as occurred during the Civil Rights Movement during the entire decade of the sixties. When he was imprisoned for several months in 1989, Christians from every walk of life—whether they fully agreed with his tactics or not—were outraged, so that even when removed from the scene, he helped to define the agenda of the church's mission to the unborn.

- Foreseeing the cataclysmic battle for life in the days to come, *Judy Brown* first became involved in the pro-life movement in 1970. Working in alternative clinics and in educational programs, her leadership abilities quickly became evident. As the public relations director of the National Right to Life Committee, she brought to the early days of the organization much needed energy and credibility. In 1977, her husband left his business career to launch the Life Amendment Political Action Committee in Washington, D.C. Shortly thereafter, Judy formed the American Life League, a research, education, communication, and public advocacy organization with a network of chapters around the nation, that has become one of the most potent forces for life today.

- One of the early pioneers of innovative pro-life activism, *Joe Schiedler* has been indefatigable in his efforts on behalf of the unborn. When the Supreme Court handed down its *Roe v. Wade* decision in 1973, he was already running the Chicago Office for Pro-Life Publicity. Later he would found the Pro-Life Action League, one of the most effective grassroots Christian ministries in the nation. Exploring virtually every avenue of child-advocacy—sponsoring sidewalk counseling, conducting seminars and rallies, holding protests and rescues, and distributing pamphlets and books—Joe's life has been a testimony of sacrifice and commitment. His landmark book, *Closed: 99 Ways to Stop Abortion,* has inspired a whole new generation of believers to develop creative strategies for the battle against the resurgent pagan child-killing industry.

- Elected to the Louisiana State Legislature in 1971 at the age of twenty-four, *Woody Jenkins* was one of the youngest legislators in this nation's history. With a wide and varied background in business, law, publishing, broadcasting, and public service, and because of his Christian convictions, in 1984 he founded Friends of the Americas—a non-profit international service organization which provides assistance to disaster victims, un-landed poor, displaced refugees, and political prisoners in twenty-two countries of Latin America. With more than seventy employees operating a hospital, seven medical clinics, a refugee center, ten schools, and innumerable self-help projects, the organization is one of the most effective relief and development ministries in the world today. Always a stalwart pro-life advocate, in both his ministry and in his legislative duties, Jenkins led Louisiana's highly visible fight in 1990 to pass the strongest abortion restrictions in the nation following the Supreme Court's *Webster* ruling.

Facing seemingly insurmountable odds, hundreds, thousands, and even millions of Christians have stood faithfully on their glorious pro-life legacy. Their stories are manifold, multifarious, and multitudinous: Charles Wysong (b. 1941), Congressman Henry Hyde (b. 1924), Curt Young

(b. 1952), John Cavenaugh-O'Keefe (b. 1950), Gary Bauer (b. 1946), Kay James (b. 1949), Paul Fowler (b. 1941), Harold O. J. Brown (b. 1933), Franky Schaeffer (b. 1952), Jerome Lejune (b. 1929), Dr. Mildred Jefferson (b. 1927), and Nellie Gray (b. 1924).

After more than twenty centuries of continuous activity, the pro-life movement is, quite obviously, alive and well.

Conclusion

Stories of valor, sacrifice, and commitment are all the more telling in times of disarray and difficulty. The great Victorian preacher, Charles Haddon Spurgeon, once said:

> If you want to comprehend a man's character, don't just watch his actions, don't simply examine his dogmas, don't merely scrutinize his living style: listen to his stories. The stories a man tells are a window to his soul.[4]

If that is true—and it seems certain that it is—then the stories of the men and women in the pro-life movement today are telling indeed. The soul that they reveal is grounded and established on, as before, five basic principles:

Orthodoxy

Whenever God's people take the Bible seriously, they inevitably begin to take seriously the sanctity of life. They inevitably begin to take seriously the call to deliver the helpless. Despite all the institutional, denominational, and theological barriers, Christians today who desire to walk in truth have joined the apostles, prophets, evangelists, martyrs, and confessors of historic orthodoxy in standing against the tide of debauchery and death.

The Church

As a single interest group, the pro-life movement has failed. As a political force, it has proven to be a total disappointment. As an institutional philanthropic enterprise, it has been more than a little impotent. But as an outreach of the historic church, it has had stunning success. The modern pro-life movement has proven that commitment to the sanctity of life is the consequence of the Spirit's work in the authentic sacramental church.

Servanthood

The crux and power of the pro-life movement today does not lie in some centralized political bureaucracy lobbying in the corridors of power. Instead, it lies in the deeds of kindness and compassion—performed in thousands of crisis pregnancy centers, unwed mothers' homes, alternative centers, shepherding homes, and mercy ministries all over the country. The power of the pro-life movement today lies in its servanthood orientation.

Urgency

More good people have suffered greater extremes of hardship and persecution for the sake of the unborn today than in any other single movement in recent memory. More Christians have sacrificed time, money, energy, reputation, and even physical welfare than anyone could ever hope to quantify. They have done this because of the more than fifty million children killed by abortion every year around the world. They have done this because the situation is urgent.

Patience

The most difficult lesson for modern Christians to learn is this one. Partially because the great legacy of the past has been forgotten for the most part—and so a bifurcation of time has taken place—and partially because we live in fast times calling for fast results and instant gratification, we find working over the long haul a very difficult task. But even here, we are learning.

❧   ❧   ❧

With sharp and perceptive wisdom, theologian R. C. Sproul has summarized the challenge that faces the contemporary church in its pro-life efforts. He said:

> The struggle against abortion is difficult, but it is worthy. The longer it lasts; the more babies will be slain. The longer laws allowing abortion-on-demand remain in effect; the more likely it is that society will be hardened in heart. Continuing the struggle against abortion is not enough. We must accelerate our efforts until no human child is destroyed under the sanction of law.[5]

He goes on to say:

> The urgency of the abortion issue requires us to protest to the very limit that our consciences allow.[6]

PART 4

THE NEXT TIME AROUND

In history's mixture of good and evil, the thing we should note—the thing the historians will note with amazement—is the profundity and the rapidity of change.
Hilaire Belloc

The oppression of the people is a terrible sin; but the depression of the people is far worse.
G. K. Chesterton

MAY THE CIRCLE BE UNBROKEN: THE LESSONS OF HISTORY

acta sanctorum [1]

The great cleavage throughout the world lies between what is with, and what is against, the faith.

Hilaire Belloc

It is an equally awful truth that four and four makes eight, whether you reckon the thing out in eight onions or eight angels, eight bricks or eight bishops, eight minor poets or eight pigs. Similarly, if it be true that God made all things, that grave fact can be asserted by pointing at a star or by waving an umbrella.

G. K. Chesterton

inston Churchill once said that, "The greatest advances in human civilization have come when we recovered what we had lost: when we learned the lessons of history."[2]

Clearly, in order to advance the cause of life and liberty in these dark and difficult days, we must recover what we have lost—we must learn the lessons of history. There is no need for us to attempt to reinvent the wheel. The pro-life battle has been fought again and again and again. Successfully. We need not cast about for direction. We need not grope in the dark for strategies, programs, and agendas. We need not manufacture new ideas, new priorities, or new tactics. We already have a tested and proven formula for victory. We already have a winning pro-life legacy. We simply need to reclaim it. We simply need to recover what is rightfully ours.

Woodrow Wilson was right on the mark when he argued that:

> A nation which does not remember what it was yesterday, does not know what it is today, nor what it is trying to do. We are trying to do a futile thing if we do not know where we came from or what we have been about. Ours is a rich legacy. Rich but lost.[3]

Interestingly, the key tenants of that lost legacy are distinctly *covenantal* in nature. The basic lessons of our long forgotten heritage conform to the Biblical pattern of *suzerianity*.[4] Thus, if we are to reclaim our legacy, we must simultaneously recover our covenantal orientation—as individuals, as families, as churches, and as a nation.

A Covenantal Legacy

The covenant is one of the most commonly misunderstood concepts in the Bible, which is terribly tragic because of the covenant's strategic Scriptural importance (see Matthew 26:28).

The covenant actually defines the pattern for the relationship between God and man (see Psalm 105:8). All of God's dealings with us are covenantal (see Psalm 25:14). He judges us covenantally (see Leviticus 26:15–16). He comforts us covenantally (see Hebrews 8:10). He fellowships with us covenantally (see Nehemiah 1:5–6). He disciplines us, rewards us, and cares for us covenantally (see Deuteronomy 28:1–68).

The covenant is actually a kind of social structure or treaty (see Romans 11:27). It brings definition and provides parameters for personal and interpersonal associations (see Galatians 3:15–29). It affords us with a pattern for all of our relationships (see 2 Corinthians 3:6). It lays the foundations for proper divine-to-human, human-to-divine, and human-to-human interaction (see Psalm 25:8–10). It is the means by which we approach, deal with, and know one another—and God (see Hebrews 13:20–21).

Through the centuries, various definitions, models, and constructs of the covenant have been conceived by theologians of every imaginable stripe. Some have taken a very straightforward trinitarian view—defining the covenant in terms of three elements.[5] Others perceive rather more complexity—defining it in terms of seven elements.[6] Still others have devised very intricate esoteric models—defining it in situationally and eschatalogically flexible terms.[7] All of these paradigms have much to commend them to the serious student of the Word, but for pedagogical purposes, we can synthesize a wide variety of their insights into five basic component parts.[8] Thus, this simplified Biblical model of the covenant begins with the establishment of God's nature and character: we must take care never to stray from basic orthodoxy because He is sovereign. Next, it proclaims God's authority: He has established order and structure in His church. Third, the covenant outlines God's ethical stipulations: He has given His people servanthood responsibilities. Fourth, it establishes God's judicial see: matters are urgent because He will one day sit in judgment. And finally, the covenant details God's very great and precious promises: we can live lives of patience because He has laid up an inheritance for the faithful.

This five-fold outline of the covenant, though by no means absolute, can be seen, in at least an oblique fashion, in God's dealings with Adam (see Genesis 1:26–31; 2:16–25), Noah (see Genesis 9:1–17), Abraham (see Genesis 12:1–3; 15:1–21), Moses (see Exodus 3:1–22), and the disciples of Christ (see 1 Corinthians 11:23–34). It is also evident in some way, shape, form, or another in the Ten Commandments (two tables of five statutes), the structure of the Pentateuch (five books), the book of Deuteronomy (five parts), the book of Psalms (five sections), the book of Revelation (five stages), and many other passages of Scripture in both the Old and New Testaments.

The pro-life movement throughout the centuries—derived as it has been from the teaching of Scripture—has invariably revolved around and has been defined in terms of the Biblical covenant. Thus, the lessons that we must learn from that legacy and the wealth that we must recover from that heritage can be summarized covenantally. Surely, if we are to have any success in the future, if we are to gain the upper hand, and if we are to faithfully contend for the sanctity of life, then we must reclaim that which we have forgotten. We must stand foursquare on the covenantal foundations laid before us: the necessity of orthodoxy, the centrality of the church, the indispensability of servanthood, the importance of decisiveness, and the primacy of patience.

Orthodoxy

Jesus is Lord. And He is Lord over the totality of life. Ultimately that means that no facet of the created order falls outside His sovereign care and direction.

Our Almighty God is both transcendent (see 1 Chronicles 29:11) and immanent (see Hebrews 13:5). He is both providential (see Isaiah 46:9–10) and immutable (see Psalm 33:8–11). He rules the cosmos, exercising His will on earth just as He does in heaven (see Psalm 147:15–18). His sovereignty encompasses the forces of creation (see Proverbs 16:4), the course of history (see Ephesians 1:11), the hearts and minds and ways of men (see Proverbs 16:9), and the workings of the nations of the earth (see Psalm 82:8).

He rules everything, everyone, and everywhere (see Psalm 135:5–7).

In light of this profound reality, the task of the believer is simply to herald the good news that "the Lord has established His throne in the heavens and His sovereignty rules over all" (Psalm 103:19). It is to acknowledge His jurisdiction over every sphere of life (see Romans 11:36). It is to affirm the validity of His decrees and precepts in every arena (see 2 Timothy 3:16–17). It is, in short, to submit to the clear-cut standards revealed in His Word (see Deuteronomy 12:32). When we say "Jesus is Lord," we must simultaneously say "Jesus is Law-Giver" (see Matthew 5:17–19). When we affirm that "Jesus is the answer," we must simultaneously affirm that "Jesus has the answers" (see John 15:10).

The word *orthodoxy* literally means adhering to the standard and acknowledging the mandates of Christ's sovereign rule. For the pro-life heroes of the past, the revelation of that "standard" or those "mandates" was very simply the Bible.

Jesus constantly reminded His disciples that the Bible was to be their only rule for life and godliness, for faith and practice, for profession and confession:

> He who has My commandments and keeps them, he it is who loves me; and he who loves me shall be loved by My Father, and I will love him, and will disclose Myself to him. If anyone loves Me, he will keep My Word; and My Father will love him, and We will come to him, and make Our abode with him. He who does not love Me does not keep My Words; and the Word which you hear is not Mine, but the Father's who sent Me. (John 14:21, 23–24)

> He said, "It is written, Man shall not live by bread alone, but by every Word that proceeds out of the mouth of God." (Matthew 4:4)

> It is easier for heaven and earth to pass away than for one tittle of the Law to fail. (Luke 16:17)

Whoever breaks one of the least of these commandments, and teaches men so, shall be called least in the
kingdom of heaven; but whoever does and teaches them
shall be called great in the kingdom of heaven. (Matthew 5:19)

Again and again, He affirmed the truth that, unlike
the ever-shifting, ever-changing fashions of men, God is
immutable:

My covenant I will not violate, nor will I alter the utter-
ance of My mouth. (Psalm 89:34)

Thus, when the Lord speaks, His Word stands firm forever. His assessments of right and wrong do not change
from age to age:

All His precepts are trustworthy. They are established forever and ever, to be performed with faithfulness and up-
rightness. (Psalm 111:7–9)

The pro-life heroes of the past knew that only too well.
That is why they relied so heavily on the Bible for the development of their priorities, agendas, strategies, and perspectives. That is why they were so careful to firmly and
forthrightly stand on the inerrant and incomparable Word.

If we are going to effectually defend the sanctity of
life—either this time around or even next time around—
then we must learn this fundamental lesson. Nothing—not
pluralistic accommodation, not high-sounding coalition
building, and not well-intentioned ecumenicism—nothing
should deter or detour us from the covenantal requisite of
orthodoxy.

The Church

Though all men are bound into a covenant with death (see
Isaiah 28:15), and though they pursue it (see Proverbs
21:6), choose it (see Jeremiah 8:3), and embrace it (see

Proverbs 2:18), deep down they desire to escape its wretched shackles (see Ecclesiastes 11:1–10).

Though they may vociferously deny it, the truth of God is written on the fleshly tablets of their hearts (see Romans 2:14–15). In fact, they must actively restrain or suppress that truth in order to carry on with their destructive ways (see Romans 1:18). Though they deliberately debase themselves with futile thinking, foolish passions, and filthy behavior, they actually know what is right (see Romans 1:19–24, 26–27). Though they consciously choose the precepts of death, they cannot escape the awful conviction of the ordinances of life (see Romans 1:28–32).

That is why all men so desperately need the church.

Only the church—as it holds steadfastly to the Word revealed, the Word made manifest, and the Word vivified—is able to effect the kind of cultural transformation necessary to snap the spell with which death grips human societies.

This is due to several great truths:

First, the church renews the minds of fallen men through the teaching of the Bible—the Word revealed. Right doctrine shatters old habits, explodes perverse ideas, and establishes real hope. The gospel changes people by the power of the Holy Spirit (see Romans 1:16). Men trapped in the snares of death and darkness need good news. They need *the* good news. And thus, God has entrusted the crucial task of publishing that good news among the nations to the church— and *only* to the church.

Second, the church readjusts men to genuine life through sacramental worship—the Word made manifest. Worship is not simply an indulgence in abstract theological rituals. Instead, it is a tangible offering *to* God, a consecration *before* God, a communion *with* God, and a transformation *before* God. In the simple yet profound act of worship, the meaning and value of life is revealed and fulfilled. It reorients men to God's plan, God's purpose, and God's program (see Psalm 73:1–28). Once again, God has entrusted this vital function to the church—and *only* to the church.

Third, the church reforms the lifestyles of men through disciple-ship—the Word vivified. The disciplined accountability of life in a local church community repatterns a man's ways according to the ways of the Lord. By instilling in them godly habits they learn "the way they should go" (Proverbs 22:16). Through ritual and repetition they are trained to walk "the paths of justice" (Proverbs 2:8) and to avoid "the ways of darkness" (Proverbs 2:13). Through routines of righteousness they are established in "every good path" (Proverbs 2:9) so that ever afterward they may "trust in the Lord with all their heart, and lean not on their own understanding, in all their ways acknowledging Him" (Proverbs 3:5–6). Thus, men are reformed through the church—and *only* through the church.

The church has the keys to the kingdom (see Matthew 16:19). It has the power to bind and loose (see Matthew 18:18). It has the authority to prevail over the very gates of hell (see Matthew 16:18). It offers men the Waters of Life (see Revelation 22:17), the Bread of Life (see John 6:35), and the Word of Life (see John 1:1), because its Head is the Author of Life (see Acts 17:25).

That is why the pro-life heroes of the past always grounded their efforts in the church. That is why they were unapologetically Christian in their advocacy of life. They knew that in order to take on the fierce dragons of death they would need the full protection and power offered in the church—and *only* in the church.

Of course, it wasn't just *any* church that these heroes for life centered their work in. It was the *one, holy, catholic, and apostolic* church.

Jesus prayed that His disciples might be *one* (see John 17:21–22). He desired for them to live in harmony. He wanted them to work together for the fuller manifestation of God's glory. In other words, He yearned for them to be *unified*.

That is what *catholicity* is—living and working together in genuine unity without backbiting, jealousy, strife, territorialism, and provincialism. It is standing as one against the tidal wave of perversity and perniciousness in the world. It is presenting a united front against the minions of death and destruction. It is:

> Being like minded, having the same love, being of one accord, and being of one mind. (Philippians 2:2)

> Attaining to the unity of faith, and of the knowledge of the Son of God, to a mature man, to the measure of the stature which belongs to the fullness of Christ. (Ephesians 4:13)

> Being diligent to preserve the unity of the Spirit in the bond of peace. For there is one body and one Spirit, just as you were also called in one hope of your calling; one Lord, one faith, one baptism, one God and Father of all who is over all and through all and in all. (Ephesians 4:3–6)

> Being of one accord and with one voice glorifying the God and Father of our Lord Jesus Christ. (Romans 15:6)

Whenever the pro-life movement has been successful throughout history, the church has been its wellspring and its mainspring. It derived its strength, its authority, its anointing, and its unction from the sacramental life of the body. The pro-life movement *was* the church. And the church *was* the pro-life movement.

If we are going to effectually defend the sanctity of life—either this time around or even next time around—then we must learn this fundamental lesson. Nothing—not the false hope of political expediency, not the hollow ideal of popular accessability, and not the deceptive allure of institutional pragmatism—nothing must be allowed to deter or detour us from the centrality of the church.

Servanthood

The gospel calls us to live *as if people really matter*. It calls us to live lives of selfless concern. We are to pay attention to the needs of others (see Deuteronomy 22:4) We are to demonstrate concern for the poor (see Psalm 41:1). We are to show pity toward the weak (see Psalm 72:13). We are to rescue the afflicted from violence (see Psalm 72:14). We are to familiarize ourselves with the case of the helpless (see Proverbs 29:7), give of our wealth (see Deuteronomy 26:12–13), and share of our sustenance (see Proverbs 22:9). We are to "put on tender mercies, kindness, humbleness of mind, meekness, and longsuffering" (Colossians 3:12). We are to become "a father to the poor," and are to search out the case of the stranger (see Job 29:16). We are to love our neighbors as ourselves (see Mark 12:31), thus fulfilling the law (see Romans 13:10).

It is only as we do these things that we are able to *earn* the right to speak authoritatively into people's lives.

In writing to Titus, the young pastor of the pioneer church on the island of Crete, the Apostle Paul pressed home this basic truth with persistence and urgency. In the midst of a culture marked by deceit, ungodliness, sloth, and gluttony (see Titus 1:12), Titus was not only to preach grace and judgment; he was also to make good deeds a central priority in his ministry. He was to exercise charity. Paul wrote:

> For the grace of God that brings salvation has appeared to all men, teaching us that, denying ungodliness and worldly lusts, we should live soberly, righteously, and godly in the present age, looking for the blessed hope and glorious appearing of our great God and Savior Jesus Christ, who gave Himself for us, that He might redeem us from every lawless deed and purify for Himself His own special people, zealous for good works. (Titus 2:11–14, NKJV)

This was a very familiar theme for Paul. It wasn't aimed exclusively at the troublesome Cretan culture. For instance, he had earlier written to the Ephesian church with essentially the same message:

> For by grace you have been saved through faith, and that not of yourselves; it is the gift of God, not of works, lest anyone should boast. For we are His workmanship, created in Christ Jesus for good works, which God prepared beforehand that we should walk in them. (Ephesians 2:8–10, NKJV)

God saves us by grace. There is nothing we can do to merit His favor. Because of our sin, we stand utterly condemned. Thus, salvation is completely unearned and undeserved. But we are not saved capriciously, for no reason and no purpose. On the contrary, we are His workmanship, created in Christ Jesus *for good works*. We are His own possession, set apart and purified to be *zealous for good works*.

In a speech before the largest single rally in our capital's history—more than a half-million pro-life Christians strong—Vice-President Dan Quayle affirmed that, "The pro-life movement is *the* humanitarian movement of our time." In point of fact, the pro-life movement has *always* been *the* humanitarian movement—throughout *all* time. Establishing charitable institutions around the globe to care for the unwanted, the unloved, and the undesired—from hospitals and orphanages to shelters and foundling centers—faithful pro-life believers have always tended the future like a garden. They were, first and foremost, servants.

If we are going to effectually defend the sanctity of life—either this time around or even next time around—then we must learn this fundamental lesson. Nothing—not the false hope of political expediancy, not the hollow ideal of popular accessibility, and not the deceptive allure of institutional pragmatism—nothing must be allowed to deter or detour us from the exigency of charitable service.

Urgency

Virtually every Biblical injunction about the Biblical use of time underlines the importance of each moment that passes. It is an ethical imperative to act and act quickly when lives are at stake, when justice is perverted, when truth is in jeopardy, when mercy is at risk, when souls are endangered, and when the gospel is assaulted.

We are admonished to "make the most of our time" (Ephesians 5:16). We are to "redeem the time" (Colossians 4:5). We are to utilize "every day to the utmost" (Hebrews 3:13). In short, we are to *sanctify* the time (see Ecclesiastes 3:1–8).

According to the Bible, our time is not our own. It is not ours to dispose of as we choose. We have been "bought with a price" (1 Corinthians 6:20). Therefore we are to set our days, weeks, and years apart to the Lord for His glory (see Romans 14:6–12).

In the Old Testament, the *days* were divided into eight distinct periods: dawn, morning, midday, dark, evening, and three night watches. These were distinguished in the lives of believers by times and seasons of prayer (see Psalm 55:17; Daniel 6:10). In the New Testament, the value of this kind of *liturgical clock* was affirmed by the followers of Christ who punctuated and accentuated their urgent task of evangelization with the discipline of regular spiritual refreshment (see Acts 3:1).

Similarly, the *weeks* of God's people were ordered with purposeful sanctity. In the Old Testament, the week centered around the Sabbath and the attendant sacrifices. In the New Testament, the week revolved around the Lord's day and the sacraments. Thus, each week had its own pace, its own schedule, its own priorities, and its own order. Thus, believers were able to give form to function and function to form (see Deuteronomy 5:12; Hebrews 10:24–25). The *liturgical calendar* enabled them to wait on the Lord and thus to "run and not be weary" and to "walk and not be faint" (Isaiah 40:31).

Even the *years* were given special structure and significance to reinforce the Biblical conception of decisive urgency. In ancient Israel, feasts, fasts, and festivals paced the community of faith in its progression through the months (see Exodus 13:6–10; Psalm 31:15). The early church continued this stewardship of time, punctuating the years with *liturgical seasons:* Advent, Christmas, Epiphany, Lent, Easter, Ascension, and Pentecost. Thus, God's people were enabled and equipped to run the race (see Philippians 2:16), to fight the fight (see Ephesians 6:10–18), to finish the course (see 2 Timothy 4:7), and to keep the faith (see 2 Timothy 3:10).

In order to maintain a sense of balanced urgency, the pro-life heroes of the past paced their efforts through the sanctification of the time. They were thus able to risk all, remain decisive, and persevere with singlemindedness. They were thus able to affirm with the psalmist:

> I hear the slander of many; fear is on every side; they counsel together against me, and they scheme to take innocent life. But as for me, I will trust in You, O my Lord; I will say, "You are my Sovereign." All my times are in Your hands. Therefore deliver me from the hand of my enemies, and from those who persecute the innocent. (Psalm 31:13–15)

Clearly, there is no room for procrastination or contemplation in times of trouble, distress, and calamity. We are called to seize the day. Decisiveness, determination, singlemindedness, constancy, diligence, and passion must inform our agenda. The pace we set should be fervent—because the task before us is urgent.

If we are going to effectually defend the sanctity of life—either this time around or even next time around— then we must learn this fundamental lesson. Nothing—not the fear for material risk, not the concern over personal reputation, and not the hesitation of institutional precedent—nothing must be allowed to deter or detour us from the indispensability of risk.

Patience

Victory will not be won in a day, however fervently we act. It will take time, perhaps generations. It has always been that way. It always will be.

In the interim, we are to rest and rely on God's "very great and precious promises" (2 Peter 1:4). We are to trust that His sovereign working will indeed make all things right (see Romans 8:28) and that His good providence will by no means be thwarted (see Ephesians 1:11).

Though the times are hard and all the earth cries out under the burden of wickedness, injustice, and perversion, we can relax in the assurance that God is playing the keys of providence according to the score of His own devising. We need not be anxious (see Philippians 4:6). We need not worry (see Matthew 6:25). We need not fret (see Luke 12: 22).

Such is the characteristic of holy patience.

Patience is actually an attribute of God Himself (see 2 Peter 3:9–15). In addition though, it is a command from on high—an non-optional mandate for every believer (see Ephesians 4:2). It is a fruit of the spirit (see Galatians 5:22). It is an evidence of love (see 1 Corinthians 13:4). It is an ensign comfort (see 2 Corinthians 1:6). And it is a qualification for church leadership (see 2 Timothy 2:24).

In times of persecution (see 1 Peter 2:20), suffering (see James 5:10), and confrontation (see 1 Thessalonians 5:14), patience is to be the Christian's overriding concern. We are to be patient in hope (see Romans 8:5). We are to be patient in affliction (see Romans 12:12). We are to be patient in our preaching (see 2 Timothy 4:2). We are to clothe ourselves in patience (see Colossians 3:12). And we are to endure in patience (see Revelation 3:12). The pace we set must be steady because the task we face will not soon be dispatched.

All through the Scriptures this lesson is emphasized:

Rest in the LORD and wait patiently for Him; do not fret because of him who prospers in his way, because of the man who carries out wicked schemes. Cease from anger, and forsake wrath; do not fret; it leads only to evil doing. For evildoers will be cut off, but those who wait for the LORD, they will inherit the land. Yet a little while and the wicked man will be no more; and you will look carefully for his place, and he will not be there. But the humble will inherit the land, and will delight themselves in abundant prosperity. (Psalm 37:7–11)

He who is slow to anger is better than the mighty, and better a patient man than a warrior who captures the city. (Proverbs 16:32)

Wisdom makes a man patient. (Proverbs 19:11a)

The end of a matter is better than its beginning; patience of spirit is better than haughtiness of spirit. Do not be eager in your heart to be angry, for anger resides in the bosom of fools. Do not say, "Why is it that the former days were better than these?" For it is not from wisdom that you ask this. Wisdom along with an inheritance is good and an advantage to those who see the sun. (Ecclesiastes 7:8–11)

By patience a ruler may be persuaded, and a soft tongue breaks the bone. (Proverbs 25:15)

According to the Bible, we are to imitate others who have manifested a spirit of patience (see Hebrews 6:12). Thus, Abraham (see Hebrews 6:13–15), Noah (see 1 Peter 3:20), and the Apostle Paul (see 2 Corinthians 6:6) are to be our models—as are the pro-life legions that have gone before us. They faced seemingly insurmountable odds with the calm assurance and the quiet confidence that could only have come from holy patience.

If we are going to effectually defend the sanctity of life—either this time around or even next time around—then we must learn this fundamental lesson. Nothing—not the urgency or immediacy of the crisis, not the horrifying specter of imminent judgment—nothing must be allowed to deter or detour us from the need for patience.

Conclusion

Pro-life efforts have been an integral aspect of the work and ministry of faithful believers since the dawning of the faith in the first century. Through all the convulsions of the patristic era, into the upheaval of the medieval epoch, on toward the Renaissance and Enlightenment, through the great missions movement and the emergence of America, and into the modern period, the *true* church has always stood for the sanctity of all innocent life—in contradistinction to the pagan consensus for abortion, infanticide, abandonment, and euthanasia. Admittedly, there have been dark days when the institutional church failed to uphold its covenantal responsibilities, but, thankfully, those days have been short-lived aberrations.

Whenever believers *have* successfully defended the helpless, their efforts have adhered to a predictable pattern—a covenantal pattern. The elements in that pattern, like the commitment to life itself, has remained remarkably consistent: an emphasis on the necessity of orthodoxy, the centrality of the church, the indispensability of servanthood, the importance of decisiveness, and the primacy of patience.

In the present struggle to uphold our two-thousand-year-old heritage, it would stand us in good stead to pay heed to this pattern—this legacy—and to reclaim it.

After all, there is no need to reinvent the wheel. As historian David R. Carlin has said:

> The best way to develop an attitude of responsibility toward the future is to cultivate a sense of responsibility toward the past. We are born into a world that we didn't make, and it is only fair that we should be grateful to those who did make it. Such gratitude carries with it the imperative that we preserve and at least slightly improve

the world that has been given us before passing it on to subsequent generations. We stand in the midst of many generations. If we are indifferent to those who went before us and actually existed, how can we expect to be concerned for the well-being of those who come after us and only potentially exist.[9]

ETERNAL VIGILANCE: HANDING ON THE LEGACY

adhuc sub judice lis est[1]

The subtle barrier was drawn which marks today from yesterday; all the night and its despondency became past and entered memory.

Hilaire Belloc

Despotism can be a development, often a late development and very often indeed the end of societies that have been very democratic. A despotism may almost be defined as a tired democracy. As fatigue falls on a community, the citizens are less inclined for that eternal vigilance which has truly been called the price of liberty.

G. K. Chesterton

he venerable aphorism remains as true today as ever: "He who forgets his own history is condemned to repeat it."[2]

Commenting on that profundity, the great Russian iconodule Aleksandr Solzhenitsyn has said that, "If we don't know our own history, we will simply have to endure all the same mistakes, sacrifices, and absurdities all over again."[3]

Further, Timothy K. Jones asserted that:

The map of God's activity is not a blank ocean between the apostolic shores and our modern day. So we need to remember—and search for our roots in—the luminaries, the risk takers, and movements of the church through the centuries. To neglect them is not only to risk repeating past errors, it is to fall victim to a narrowing amnesia that leaves us floundering.[4]

Our Sense of History

It seems that in this awkward new epoch we are afflicted with a malignant contemporaneity. Our morbid preoccupation with ourselves—and thus our ambivalence and ignorance of the past—has trapped us in a recalcitrant present. Renowned historian Daniel Boorstin has said:

> In our schools today, the story of our nation has been replaced by *social studies*—which is the study of what ails us *now*. In our churches, the effort to see the essential nature of man has been displaced by the *social gospel*— which is the polemic against the pet vices of *today*. Our book publishers no longer seek the timeless and the durable, but spend most of their efforts in a fruitless search for—*la mode social commentary*—which they pray will not be out of date when the item goes to press. Our merchandisers frantically devise their new year models, which will cease to be voguish when their sequels appear three months hence. Neither our classroom lessons nor our sermons nor our books nor the things we live with nor the houses we live in are any longer strong ties to our past. We have become a nation of short-term doomsayers. In a word, we have lost our sense of history. Without the materials of historical comparison, we are left with nothing but abstractions.[5]

History is not just the concern of historians and social scientists. It is not the lonely domain of political prognosticators and ivory tower academics. It is the very stuff of life. And it is the very stuff of faith. In fact, the Bible puts a *heavy* emphasis on historical awareness—not at all surprising considering the fact that the vast proportion of its own contents record the dealings of God with men and nations throughout the ages.

Again and again in the Scriptures, God calls upon His people to *remember*. He calls on us to remember the bondage, oppression, and deliverance of Egypt (see Exodus 13:3; Deuteronomy 6:20–23). He calls on us to remember the splendor, strength, and devotion of the Davidic kingdom (see 1 Chronicles 16:8–36). He calls on us to remember the valor, forthrightness, and holiness of the prophets (see James 5:7–11). He calls on us to remember the glories of creation (see Psalm 104:1–30), the devastation of the flood (see 2 Peter 2:4–11), the judgment of the great apostasies (see Jude 5–11), the miraculous events of the exodus (see Deuteronomy 5:15), the anguish of the desert wanderings (see Deuteronomy 8:1–6), the grief of the Babylonian exile (see Psalm 137:1–6), the responsibility of the restoration (see Ezra 9:5–15), the sanctity of the Lord's Day (see Exodus 20:8), the graciousness of the commandments (see Numbers 15:39–40), and the ultimate victory of the cross (see 1 Corinthians 11:23–26). He calls on us to remember the lives and witness of all those who have gone before us in faith—forefathers, fathers, patriarchs, prophets, apostles, preachers, evangelists, martyrs, confessors, ascetics, and every righteous spirit made pure in Christ (see 1 Corinthians 10:1–11; Hebrews 11:3–40).

He calls on us to *remember*. As the psalmist has said:

> We must remember the deeds of the LORD in our midst. Surely, we must remember His wonders of old. I will meditate on all Your work, and muse on Your deeds. Your way is holy; what god is like unto our God? You are the God who works wonders; You have made known Your strength among the peoples. You have by power redeemed Your people, the sons of Jacob and Joseph. (Psalm 77:11–15)

And again:

Oh give thanks to the LORD, call upon His name. Make
known His deeds among the peoples. Sing to Him, sing
praises to Him; speak of all His wonders on the earth.
Glory in His name; let the heart of those who seek the
Lord be glad. Seek the Lord and His strength; seek His
face continually. Remember His wonders which He has
done in our midst, His marvels and the judgments uttered by His mouth. (Psalm 105:1–5)

When Moses stood before the Israelites at the end of
his long life, he did not exhort them with polemics or mor-
alisms. He reminded them of the works of God in history.
He reminded them of their duty to *remember* (see Deuteronomy 32:1–43).

When David stood before his family and friends following a great deliverance from his enemies, he did not stir
them with sentiment or nostalgia. He reminded them of the
works of God in history in a psalm of praise. He reminded
them of their duty to *remember* (see 2 Samuel 22:1–51).

When Solomon stood before his subjects at the dedica-
tion of the newly constructed temple, he did not challenge
them with logic or rhetoric. He simply reminded them of the
works of God in history in a hymn of wisdom. He reminded
them of their duty to *remember* (see 1 Kings 8:15–61).

When Nehemiah stood before the families of Jerusalem
at the consecration of the rebuilt city walls, he did not
bombard them with theology or theatrics. He simply reminded them of the works of God in history in a song of
the covenant. He reminded them of their duty to *remember*
(see Nehemiah 9:6–38).

When Stephen stood before an accusing and enraged
Sanhedrin, he did not confront them with apology or condemnation. He simply reminded them of the works of God
in history in a litany of faith. He reminded them of their
duty to *remember* (see Acts 7:2–53).

Remembrance and forgetfulness are the measuring
rods of faithfulness throughout the entire canon of Scripture. A family that passes its legacy on to its children will

bear great fruit (see Deuteronomy 8:2–10). A family that
fails to take its heritage seriously will remain barren (see
Deuteronomy 8:11–14). A people that remembers the great
and mighty deeds of the Lord will be blessed (see Deuteronomy 8:18). A people that forgets is doomed to frustration
and failure (see Deuteronomy 8:19–20). In fact, the whole
direction of a culture depends on the gracious appoint-
ments of memory:

> Wonders cannot be known in the midst of darkness.
> Righteousness cannot be done in a land of forgetfulness.
> (Psalm 88:12)

That is why the Bible makes it plain that there are only
two kinds of people in the world: effectual doers and for-
getful hearers (see James 1:25). And that is why the ministry of the Holy Spirit in the lives of believers is primarily to
bring to our *remembrance* the Word of Truth (see John
14:26).

Philip Schaff, the prolific church historian during the
previous generation, argued stridently that we must be eter-
nally vigilant in the task of handing on our great legacy—
to remember and then to inculcate that remembrance in
the hearts and minds of our children:

> How shall we labor with any effect to build up the
> church, if we have no thorough knowledge of its history,
> or fail to apprehend it from the proper point of observa-
> tion? History is, and must ever continue to be, next to
> God's Word, the richest foundation of wisdom, and the
> surest guide to all successful practical activity.[6]

Indeed, in this ongoing epic struggle for life—in this
tortured clash between historic Christianity and ancient paganism—we dare not neglect our rich legacy. And we dare
not keep it to ourselves:

> Listen, oh my people, to my instruction; incline your
> ears to the words of my mouth. I will open my mouth in
> a parable; I will utter dark sayings of old, which we have

heard and known, and our fathers have told us. We will not conceal them from our children, but tell to the generation to come the praises of the LORD, and His strength and His wondrous works that He has done. For He established a testimony in our midst and appointed a new law in the land, which He commanded to our fathers, that they should teach them to their children that the generation to come might know, even the children yet to be born that they may in turn arise and tell them to their children, that they should put their confidence in God, and not forget the works of God, but keep His commandments. (Psalm 78:1–7)

Conclusion

Clearly, we stand at a crossroads in our culture today. But then, we've been here before. During the crucial final days of his 1912 presidential campaign—at another of the great American crossroads—Theodore Roosevelt challenged the nation with typical prophetic fervor to recapture its legacy—and then pass it on:

Just beyond man's narrow daily vision stand the immortals. *"And Jehovah opened the eyes of the young man, and he saw; and, behold, the mountain was full of horses and chariots about Elisha."* At the front of this culture's way ride the strong guards of our own past, their authority immortalized by faithfulness. In the hour of decision we see them; their grave eyes watch us, the keepers of our standards, the builders of our civilization. They came from God to do his bidding and returned. The future we cannot see; nor what the next imperious task; nor who its strong executant. But for this generation, in a time charged with disintegrating forces, the challenge is clear: to uphold our legacy with faith, valor, and truth.[7]

He concluded by saying:

Now to you men who in your turn have come together to spend and be spent in the endless crusade against wrong, to you who gird yourselves for this great fight in the never-ending warfare for the good of mankind, I say in closing, *"We stand at Armageddon and we battle for the Lord."* [8]

Would to God that—across the wide span of the intervening decades—we would hear and heed. Amen and Amen.

NOTES

Introduction: Round and Round

1. Actions speak louder than words.
2. Quoted in Martin Forbes, *History Lessons: The Importance of Cultural Memory* (New York: Palamir Publications, 1981), 61.
3. Quoted in Tim Dowley, ed., *Eerdmans' Handbook to the History of Christianity* (Grand Rapids, MI: Wm. B. Eerdmans Publishing Co., 1977), 2.
4. Ibid.

Chapter One: In the Valley of the Shadow of Death: An Anthropology

1. One misstep leads to another.
2. The full range of human passion and its exegetical manipulation in literature has been a subject of especial concern to my colleague, Dr. Addison Soltau. I am indebted to him for his searching insights into this provocative subject.
3. *Didache,* 1.1.

Chapter Two: How Firm a Foundation: The Apostolic Church

1. From greatest to least.
2. Although the Valenzia name does not appear in any historical records until near the end of the eleventh century when the largest part of the family moved to Venice, I have used it throughout for simpler identification purposes.
3. *Canons,* 188.2.
4. *Code of Justinian,* 8.52.2.
5. *Didache,* 1.1; 2.2.
6. *Epistle of Barnabas,* 19.5.
7. *A Plea for the Christians,* 35.6.
8. *Paedagogus,* 2.10.96.

9. *Apology,* 8.6; 9.4.

10. *Hexameron,* 5.16.58.

11. *Letter to Eustochium,* 22.13.

12. *On Marriage,* 1.17.15.

Chapter Three: A New Consensus: The Medieval Church

1. From start to finish.

2. *Hagia Damhait,* 3.15.

3. The brilliant academic apologist for homosexuality and abortion from Yale University, John Boswell, has written a stunning refutation of this centuries old contention in his book, *The Kindness of Strangers: The Abandonment of Children in Western Europe from Late Antiquity to the Renaissance* (New York: Pantheon Books, 1988).

   Though his research into primary source documents is comprehensive and his mastery of the material is obvious, Boswell succumbs to the tempting impulse of forcing the facts to fit his own libertine presuppositions. The result is an impressive display of creative historical revisionism: the reason that the medieval church took such great pains to care for the abandoned and even institutionalized oblation, according to Boswell, was simply to keep a steady stream of recruits and cheap labor flowing into the monastery system. That is *prima facie* absurd.

   Thus, despite the fact that he has done the academic community a great service by tracking down innumerable obscure documents—many of which I have actually used in this study—the ultimate value of Boswell's work is diminished greatly by the twisted propaganda techniques that he used to draw his conclusions.

4. *Code of Justinian,* 18.51–52.

5. *Patrologia: Series Latina,* 84.262.

6. *Concilia Galliae,* 7.884.

7. *Decretorum Libri,* 3.200–202.

8. *Decretum,* 3.252–254.

9. Ivo, *Decretum,* 8.318; quoted verbatim in Gratian, *Decretum,* 1.306.

Chapter Four: Castles in the Air: The Renaissance and the Enlightenment

1. Through difficulties to honors.

2. Quoted in Jean-Marc Anoulih, *Monsieur Vincent* (Paris: Delarge Press, 1928), 98–99.

3. John Calvin, trans. Charles Bingham, *Calvin's Commentaries* (Grand Rapids, MI: Baker Book House, 1981), 3:42.

4. John Calvin, in "The Sum of the Christian Life: The Denial of Ourselves," trans. John T. McNeil, *The Institutes of the Christian Religion: The Four Volume Classroom Edition* (Philadelphia: Westminster Press, 1962), 348.

5. Lambert Collier, *The Jesuits: The Warrior Priests of the Pope* (New York: Maethan Brothers Publishing, 1926), 87.

6. The difference between the abolitionist movement in England—which was led for the most part by pious and committed evangelical Christians—and the abolitionist movement in the northern United States—which was led for the most part by revolutionary and anti-Christian Unitarian Socialists—was quite profound, as might be expected by their divergent philosophical roots.

7. As defined in the Seven Ecumenical Councils and the Creeds of Antiquity, as well as the confessions of the reformation such as the Canons of Dort, the Augsburg Confession, the Diet of Worms, the Belgic Confession, and Westminster Confession.

Chapter Five: To the Uttermost: The Great Missions Movement

1. In this sign you shall conquer.

2. Anna Bowden, *Missionary Journals* (London: Sunday Schools Association for Overseas Missions, 1896), 1:11.

3. Ibid., 135.

4. Ibid.

5. Ibid.

6. This phrase is appropriately used by pro-abortionist lawyer Lawrence Tribe as a subtitle in his remarkable book, *Abortion: The Clash of Absolutes* (New York: W. W. Norton, 1990). Although unhesitatingly and uncompromisingly committed to the cause of child-killing, Tribe, a well-known professor of constitutional law at Harvard, is forced to admit that abortion can only be advocated by those who have jettisoned the last remaining remnants of Biblical orthodoxy. He essentially—and accurately—defines the titanic struggle between pro-lifers and "pro-choicers" as the struggle between Christian absolutes and pagan absolutes.

7. Quoted in William Robert Boyle, *An Empire of Good: The Impact of the Gospel on the Modern World* (Atlanta, GA: Reaching the Nations Press, 1981), 11.

8. In comprehending the impact of the missions movement in the nineteenth century on heathen cultures, the work of Thomas Sowell

in his book *Preferential Policies: An International Perspective* (New York: William Morrow, Publishers, 1990) is indispensible. The book surveys various times and places where particular races have received special treatment under law—either negatively or positively.

In a chapter entitled, "Majority Preferences in Minority Economies," Sowell analyzes countries where minority groups have aroused the envy of the majority by achieving at a significantly higher rate. In Nigeria, for example, the majority northern tribes were and are Muslim. During the period of British colonial rule, missionaries were legally confined to ministry among the minority in the south. According to Sowell, "The net result was that education and hospitals, among other features of Western culture, were concentrated among the peoples of southern Nigeria." When the British left, the Ibos of the south completely dominated the positions of power and prestige in both the public and private sphere. The northern majority voted themselves "affirmative action" programs and provoked a civil war in an attempt to balance the obvious discrepancies (pp. 69–76). Again, in Sri Lanka, multi-cultural harmony was carefully preserved under British rule. The Buddhist Sinhalese majority, however, remained resistant to Christian missions—particularly missionary schools. The Tamil minority learned English and pursued various avenues of upward mobility. In the end the Tamils occupied the vast majority of the higher positions in the post-colonial society (76–87).

The point of all this? Sowell argues that Nigeria and Sri Lanka—as well as a number of other examples from Indonesia to Brazil—clearly illustrate the tremendous impact that Christian missions have made to the social, legal, and economic structure of pagan cultures around the world. And they illustrate the gracious benefit that the seamless ethic of pro-education, pro-health, pro-work, pro-development, pro-family, and pro-life values affect the everyday life of formerly oppressed and impoverished peoples.

9. Quoted in Charles Morris, *The Marvelous Record of the Closing Century* (Philadelphia: American Book and Bible House, 1899), 610.

10. Ibid.

11. James S. Dennis, *Christian Missions and Social Progress* (Old Tappan, NJ: Revell, 1909), 2:130.

12. Ibid., 347.

13. David Livingstone, *Missionary Travels and Researches in Southern Africa* (New York: Eglund and Wilson Publishers, 1952), xii–xiii.

14. Dennis, 302.

15. J. H. Gordon, ed., *Heralds of the Great Commission* (Richmond, VA: Missions Annual Publication Society, 1911), 132.

Chapter Six: Life and Liberty: The American Experience

1. The die is cast.

2. Quoted in Marvin Olasky, *The Press and Abortion, 1838–1988* (Hillsdale, NJ: Lawrence Erlbaum Associates, Publishers, 1988), 26.

3. Ibid.

4. Ibid., 27.

5. Ibid., 28.

6. Ibid.

7. Ibid.

8. Ibid., 27.

9. James Macaulay, *Current Heroes: Examples of Faith for Our Time* (New York: American Tract Society, 1879), 56–57.

10. Marvin Laddler, ed., *The St. Clair Clan* (New York: Laddler's Geniological Guide Books, n.d.), 23.

11. Macaulay, 36–39.

12. Ibid., 29.

13. Ibid.

14. Ibid., 42.

15. See David M. Kennedy, *Birth Control in America: The Career of Margaret Sanger* (New Haven, CT: Yale University Press, 1970), 36–71.

16. James C. Mohr, *Abortion in America: The Origins and Evolution of National Policy* (New York: Oxford University Press, 1978), 221–224.

17. Ibid.

18. Quoted in *The Boston Pilot,* December 11, 1869.

19. E. Frank Howe, *Sermon on Ante-Natal Infanticide* (Terra Haute, IN: Allen and Andrews, 1869), 2.

20. Reported in *The Christian Mirror,* August 4, 1868.

21. Ibid.

22. *Minutes of the General Assembly of the Presbyterian Church in the United States of America, XVIII* (Philadelphia: Presbyterian Publications Committee, 1869), 937.

23. Quoted in *The Christian Monitor,* July 18, 1868.

24. Ibid.

25. *The Revolution,* July 8, 1869.

26. Letter to Julia Ward Howe, October 16, 1878.

27. *The Revolution,* April 9, 1868.

28. Thomas Paine, *Common Sense and Other Essays* (New York: Signet Classics, 1977), 19.

29. Harold K. Lane, *Liberty! Cry Liberty!* (Boston: Lamb and Lamb Tractarian Society, 1939), 31.

30. Abraham Lincoln, *Speeches, Letters, and Papers: 1860–1864* (Washington, DC: Capitol Library, 1951), 341–342.

31. Quoted in John W. Whitehead, *The Separation Illusion* (Milford, MI: Mott Media, 1977), 21.

Chapter Seven: Abominations and Admonitions: The Making of Modernism

1. How quickly we forget.

2. Theodore Roosevelt, *Foes of Our Own Household* (New York: Charles Scribner's Sons, 1917, 1926), 3.

3. Quoted in Harold Tribble Cole, *The Coming Terror: Life Before the Great War* (New York: Languine Bros., Publishers, 1936), 21.

4. Ibid.

5. Ibid.

6. Ibid., 23.

7. Quoted in Noah Brooks, *Men of Achievement: Statesmen* (New York: Charles Scribner's Sons, 1904), 317.

8. Quoted in David L. Johnson, *Theodore Roosevelt: American Monarch* (Philadelphia: American History Sources, 1981), 44.

9. Ibid.

10. Roosevelt, 152.

11. See Kennedy, *Birth Control,* 146–147.

12. Ibid., 47.

13. Roosevelt, 7.

14. Ibid., 167

15. *The Woman Rebel,* May 1914.

16. Ibid.

17. Ibid.

18. Robert M. Crunden, *Ministers of Reform: The Progressives' Achievement in American Civilization, 1889–1920* (New York: Basic Books, 1982), 3.

19. Cited in Alan Chase, *The Legacy of Malthus: The Social Costs of the New Scientific Racism* (New York: Alfred Knopf, 1977), 7.

20. Quoted in Lawrence S. Pavallon, *Fascists, Marxists, Dictators, and Petty Tyrants: Oppressive Social Policies in the Twentieth Century* (London: Western Outpost Publications Centre, 1979), 71.

21. Ibid.

22. Ibid., 96.

23. Ibid.

24. See George Grant, *Grand Illusions: The Legacy of Planned Parenthood* (Brentwood, TN: Wolgemuth & Hyatt, Publishers, Inc. 1988).

25. Margaret Sanger, *The Pivot of Civilization* (New York: Brentano's, 922), 23.

26. Ibid., 176.

27. Ibid., 108.

28. Committee on Marriage and the Home of the Federal Council of Churches of Christ in America, *Moral Aspects of Birth Control* (New York: FCC Publications, 1931).

29. *New York Times,* December 16, 1935.

30. Quoted in, Religious Coalition for Abortion Rights, *We Affirm* (Washington, DC: Religious Coalition for Abortion Rights Educational Fund, 1989), 7.

31. Ibid.

32. Ibid., 1.

33. Ibid.

34. Ibid., 3.

35. *Christianity Today,* November 8, 1968.

36. G. K. Chesterton, *Eugenics and Other Evils* (London: Cassell, 1922), 7.

37. Ibid., 54.

38. *The Speaker,* February 2, 1901.

39. Chesterton, *Eugenics,* 151.

40. Henri de Lubac, *Christian Resistance to Anti-Semitism: Memories from 1940–1944* (San Francisco: St. Ignatius Press, 1990), 28.

41. Ibid., 32–33.

42. Ibid., 34.

43. Ibid., 121, note.

44. Quoted in Robert J. Lifton, *The Nazi Doctors: Medical Killing and the Psychology of Genocide* (New York: Basic Books, 1986), 93–94.

45. Ibid., 94.

46. Ibid.

47. Ruth A. Tucker, *Guardians of the Great Commission: The Story of Women in Modern Missions* (Grand Rapids, MI: Zondervan, 1988), 134.

48. Hunter B. Blakely, *Religion in Shoes* (Birmingham, AL: Southern University Press, 1989), 190–191.

49. Ibid.

50. Edgar Allan Poe, *Complete Works* (New York: Student's Library, 1966), 48.

Chapter Eight: Rescue the Perishing: The New Pro-Life Emergence

1. Where there is life, there is hope.

2. *Moody Monthly,* May 1980.

3. Charles R. Swindoll, *Sanctity of Life: The Inescapable Issue* (Dallas, TX: Word Publishing, 1990), xiv.

4. Quoted in Michael T. Ramey, *Spurgeon: The Philanthropist* (Kansas City, MO: Calvinist Baptist Publication Society, 1951), 165.

5. R. C. Sproul, *Abortion: A Rational Look at an Emotional Issue* (Colorado Springs, CO: NavPress, 1990), 156.

6. Ibid.

Chapter Nine: May the Circle Be Unbroken: The Lessons of History

1. The deeds of the saints.

2. Quoted in Martin Forbes, *History Lessons: The Importance of Cultural Memory* (New York, Palamir Publications, 1981), 61.

3. Quoted in Calvin Long, *The Progressive Era: The Roaring Nineties to the Roaring Twenties* (New York: Birch Tree Press, 1958), 146.

4. A *suzerian* was a tribal chieftan in the ancient Middle East. Thus, the pattern of *suzerianity* is the treaty structure that those chieftans imposed on conquered territories. Such treaties established 1) who was in authority; 2) how the society was to be ordered; 3) what the code of ethics would be; 4) how judgment was to be exacted; and 5) how succession or inheritance was to be arranged.

5. For a delightful historical sightseeing tour of this view—and its implications in ecclesiology—see Allen A. Ferrar, *The Trinitarian Covenant: An Overview Through the Centuries* (Oxford, UK: Campus Publications Society, 1979).

6. For the comparative merits of the different models, see Meredith Kline, *Treaty of the Great King: The Covenant Structure of Deuteronomy* (Grand Rapids, MI: Wm. B. Eerdmans Publishing Co., 1963); and

Ray Sutton, *That You May Prosper* (Fort Worth, TX: Dominion Press, 1987).

7. See, for example, Claus Westermann, *The Living Psalms* (Grand Rapids, MI: Wm. B. Eerdmans Publishing Company, 1989); Edward F. Campbell, *Ruth,* The Anchor Bible series, (Garden City, NY: Doubleday and Company, 1975); and Mitchell Dahood, *Psalms,* 3 vols., in The Anchor Bible series (Garden City, NY: Doubleday and Company, 1976, 1979).

8. None of the models are universal—fitting every Scriptural circumstance—but it seems to me that the five-point pattern is a helpful teaching tool and that it covers most of the covenantal contingencies.

9. David R. Carlin, *Church History,* 9:1, February 1990.

Chapter Ten: Eternal Vigilance: Handing on the Legacy

1. The case is still before the court.

2. Michael Laughton-Douglas, *Truer Truth Than This: A Philosophical Inquiry into Epistomology and Ranology During the Medieval Epoch* (London: Haverford Bookstall, Ltd., 1978), 84.

3. Ibid.

4. Carlin, *Church History,* 9:1, February 1990.

5. *Newsweek,* July 6, 1970.

6. Carlin, *Church History,* 9:1, February 1990.

7. Quoted in David L. Johnson, *Theodore Roosevelt: American Monarch* (Philadelphia: American History Sources, 1981), 103.

8. Ibid.

BIBLIOGRAPHIC RESOURCES

Airès, Philippe, and Georges Duby, eds. *A History of Private Life.* 5 vols. Cambridge, MA: The Belknap Press, 1989.

Alcorn, Randy. *Is Rescuing Right? Breaking the Law to Save the Unborn.* Downers Grove, IL: InterVarsity Press, 1990.

Andrews, Joan, with John Cavanaugh-O'Keefe. *I Will Never Forget You: The History of the Rescue Movement in the Life of Joan Andrews.* San Francisco: St. Ignatius Press, 1989.

Andrews, Joan. *You Reject Them, You Reject Me: The Prison Letters of Joan Andrews.* Brentwood, TN: Wolgemuth & Hyatt, Publishers, Inc., 1988.

Andrusko, Dave. *To Rescue the Future: The Pro-Life Movement in the 1980's.* Harrison, NY: Life Cycle Books, 1983.

Andrusko, Dave. *Window on the Future: The Pro-Life Year in Review—1986.* Washington, DC: The National Right-To-Life Committee, 1987.

Ankerberg, John, and John Weldon. *When Does Life Begin? And 39 Other Tough Questions About Abortion.* Brentwood, TN: Wolgemuth & Hyatt, Publishers, Inc., 1989.

Anoulih, Jean-Marc. *Monsieur Vincent.* Paris: Delarge Press, 1928.

Aramony, William. *The United Way: The Next Hundred Years.* New York: Donald I. Fine, 1987.

Athanasius. *On the Incarnation.* Crestwood, NY: St. Vladimir's Seminary Press, 1944.

Attwater, Donald. *Dictionary of the Saints.* Updated and revised by Catherine Rachel John. London: Penguin Books, 1983.

Bacon, Francis. *The Essays.* New York: Penguin Books, 1985.

Bajema, Clifford. *Abortion and the Meaning of Personhood.* Grand Rapids, MI: Baker Book House, 1974.

Banks, J. A. and Olive. *Feminism and Family Planning in Victorian England: Studies in the Life of Women.* New York: Schocken Books, 1964.

Bannan, Alfred J., and Achilles Edelenyi. *Documentary History of Eastern Europe.* New York: Twayne Publishers, 1970.

Belloc, Hilaire. *The Cruise of the Nona.* London: Constable and Co., Ltd., 1925.

Belloc, Hilaire. *The Four Men: A Farrago.* Oxford: Oxford University Press, 1912.

Belloc, Hilaire. *Notes of a Curmudgeon.* London: Albright's Ltd., 1956.

Belloc, Hilaire. *The Path to Rome.* London: Penguin Books, 1902.

Belloc, Hilaire. *Survivals and New Arrivals.* London: Duckworth and Company, 1929.

Beltz, Mark. *Suffer the Little Children: Christians, Abortion and Civil Disobedience.* Westchester, IL: Crossway Books, 1989.

Berry, Dr. Caroline. *The Rites of Life: Christians and Bio-Medical Decision Making.* London: Hodder and Stoughton, 1987.

Billington, James H. *Fire in the Minds of Men: Origins of the Revolutionary Faith.* New York: Basic Books, 1980.

Binding, Karl. *The Release of the Destruction of Life Devoid of Value.* Santa Ana, CA: Life Quality, 1975.

Bosgra, T. *Abortion, the Bible, and the Church.* Honolulu, HI: Hawaii Right-To-Life Educational Foundation, 1980.

The Boston Women's Health Collective. *The New Our Bodies, Our Selves: A Book by and for Women.* New York: Simon and Schuster, 1984.

Boswell, John. *The Kindness of Strangers: the Abandonment of Children in Western Europe from Late Antiquity to the Renaissance.* New York: Pantheon Books, 1988.

Brennan, William. *Medical Holocausts: Exterminative Medicine in Nazi Germany and Contemporary America.* New York: Nordland, 1980.

Brooks, Jim. *Origins of Life.* Belville, MI: Lion Publishing Corporation, 1985.

Brown, Peter. *Society and the Holy in Late Antiquity.* London: Faber and Faber, 1982.

Burgwyn, Diana. *Marriage Without Children.* New York: Harper and Row, 1981.

Buzzard, Lynn, and Paula Campbell. *Holy Disobedience: When Christians Must Resist the State.* Ann Arbor, MI: Servant Books, 1984.

Calvin, John. *Calvin's Commentaries.* Translated by Charles Bingham. Grand Rapids, MI: Baker Book House, 1981.

Carr, Steven A., and Franklin A. Meyer. *Celebrate Life: Hope for a Culture Preoccupied with Death.* Brentwood, TN: Wolgemuth & Hyatt, Publishers, Inc., 1990.

Cartier, Roger. *Passions of the Renaissance.* Vol. 3 of A History of Private Life. Cambridge, MA: Belknap Press, 1989.

Cartwright, F. F. *A Social History of Medicine.* London: Longman House, 1977.

Catholic Media Office and Incorporated Catholic Truth Society. *Abortion and the Right to Live: A Joint Statement of the Catholic Archbishops of Great Britain.* London: The Ludo Press Ltd., 1986.

Catholic Truth Society. *Let Me Live: Declaration by the Sacred Congregation of Faith on Procured Abortion.* London: Burleigh Press, 1983.

Chadwick, J., and W. N. Mann, eds. *Hippocratic Writings.* London: Penguin Books, 1950.

Chadwick, Owen. *The Reformation*. London: Penguin Books, 1964.

Chambers, Claire. *The Siecus Circle: A Humanist Revolution*. Belmont, MA: Western Islands, 1977.

Chase, Allan. *The Legacy of Malthus: The Social Costs of the New Scientific Racism*. New York: Alfred A. Knopf, 1975.

Chastain, Jane. *I'd Speak Out on the Issues If I Only Knew What to Say*. Ventura, CA: Regal Books, 1987.

Chesterton, G. K. *Collected Works: Volume XXVIII: The Illustrated London News 1908–1910*. San Francisco, CA: St. Ignatius Press, 1987.

Chesterton, G. K. *The Everlasting Man*. New York: Dodd, Mead, and Company, 1925.

Chesterton, G. K. *G. K. C. as M. C.* London: Methuen and Co., 1929.

Chesterton, G. K. *Orthodoxy*. Garden City, NY: Image Books, 1959.

Chesterton, G. K. *The Quotable Chesterton*. Ed. by George Marlin, Richard P. Rabatin, and John L. Swan. Garden City, NY: Image Books, 1987.

Chesterton, G. K. *Saint Thomas Aquinas: The Dumb Ox*. Garden City, NY: Image Books, 1956.

Christian, S. Rickly. *The Woodland Hills Tragedy*. Westchester, IL: Crossway Books, 1985.

Clark, Colin. *Population Growth: The Advantages*. Santa Ana, CA: Life Quality, 1975.

Coakley, Mary Lewis. *Long Liberated Ladies*. San Francisco, CA: St. Ignatius Press, 1987.

Collier, Lambert. *The Jesuits: The Warrior Priests of the Pope*. New York: Methan Brothers Publishing, 1926.

Colson, Charles. *The God of Stones and Spiders: Letters to a Church in Exile*. Wheaton, IL: Crossway Books, 1990.

Committee on Population and the Economy. *Getting Population into Perspective.* London: The SPUC Educational Research Trust, 1987.

Corrin, Jay P. *G. K. Chesterton and Hilaire Belloc: The Battle Against Modernity.* London: Ohio University Press, 1981.

Cragg, Gerald R. *The Church and the Age of Reason: 1648-1789.* London: Pelican Books, 1960.

Cruden, Robert M. *Ministers of Reform: The Progressives' Achievement in American Civilization, 1889–1920.* New York: Basic Books, 1982.

Curtis, Lindsay R., Glade B. Curtis, and Mary K. Beard. *My Body-My Decision.* New York: Signet, 1987.

Cutts, E. L. *Christians Under the Crescent in Asia.* New York: Pott, Young and Co., 1912.

Davis, John Jefferson. *Abortion and the Christian: What Every Christian Should Know.* Phillipsburg, NJ: Presbyterian and Reformed, 1984.

Davis, Dr. Ron Lee with James D. Denney. *A Time for Compassion: A Call to Cherish and Protect Life.* Old Tappan, NJ: Revell, 1986.

de Lubac, Henri. *Christian Resistance to Anti-Semitism: Memories from 1940–1944.* San Francisco, CA: St. Ignatius Press, 1990.

DeJong, Peter, and William Smit. *Planning Your Family: How To Decide What's Best for You.* Grand Rapids, MI: Zondervan, 1987.

Dennis, James S. *Christian Missions and Social Progress.* Vol. I and II. Old Tappan, NJ: Revell, 1909.

deParrie, Paul, and Mary Pride. *Ancient Empires of the New Age.* Westchester, IL: Crossway Books, 1989.

deParrie, Paul, and Mary Pride. *Unholy Sacrifices of the New Age.* Westchester, IL: Crossway Books, 1988.

Dinnage, Rosemary. *Annie Besant.* London: Penguin Books, 1986.

Doherty, Dr. Peter. *Abortion: Is This Your Choice?* London: Faith Pamphlets, 1982.

Douglas, J. D., Walter A. Elwell, and Peter Toon. *The Concise Dictionary of the Christian Tradition: Doctrine, Liturgy, and History.* Grand Rapids, MI: Zondervan, 1989.

Dowley, Tim, ed. *Eerdman's Handbook to the History of Christianity.* Grand Rapids, MI: Wm. B. Eerdman's Publishing Co., 1977.

Downs, Robert B. *Books That Changed the World.* New York: Mentor Books, 1983.

Drexler, Eric K. *Engines of Creation: The Coming Era of Nanotechnology.* New York: Anchor Press/ Doubleday, 1987.

Drogin, Elasah. *Margaret Sanger: Father of Modern Society.* New Hope, KY: CUL Publishers, 1980, 1986.

Duby, Georges. *Revelations of the Medieval World.* Vol. 2 of A History of Private Life. Cambridge, MA: Belknap Press, 1988.

Dwight, Rev. Henry Otis., Rev. H. Allen Tupper, and Rev. Edwin Munsell Bliss. *The Encyclopedia of Missions.* New York: Funk and Wagnalls Co., 1904.

Eisenstein, Zillah. *The Radical Future of Liberal Feminism.* New York: Longman Co., 1981.

Elliot, Elisabeth. *A Chance to Die: The Life and Legacy of Amy Carmichael.* Old Tappan, NJ: Revell, 1987.

Ellis, William. *Journal of William Ellis.* Tokyo: Tuttle, 1827.

Espinosa, J. C. *Birth Control: Why Are They Lying to Women?* Washington, DC: Human Life International, 1980.

Evans, Debra. *Without Moral Limits: Women, Reproduction and the New Medical Technology.* Westchester, IL: Crossway Books, 1989.

Exley, Richard. *Abortion: Pro-Life by Conviction, Pro-Choice by Default.* Tulsa, OK: Honor Books, 1989.

Farmer, David Hugh. *The Oxford Dictionary of Saints.* New York: Oxford University Press, 1987.

Faux, Marian. *Crusaders: Voices from the Abortion Front.* New York: Birch Lane Press, 1990.

Faux, Marian. *Roe v. Wade: The Untold Story of the Landmark Supreme Court Decision That Made Abortion Legal.* New York: Macmillan Publishing Co., 1988.

Fleming, William. *Art, Music and Ideas.* New York: Holt, Rinehart and Winston, 1969.

Fletcher, Joseph. *Situation Ethics: The New Morality.* Philadelphia, PA: The Westminster Press, 1966.

Forbes, Martin. *History Lessons: The Importance of Cultural Memory.* New York: Palamir Publications, 1981.

Fowler, Paul B. *Abortion: Toward an Evangelical Consensus.* Portland, OR: Multnomah Press, 1987.

Fox, Robin Lane. *Pagans and Christians.* New York: Alfred A. Knopf, 1987.

Frame, John M. *Medical Ethics: Principles, Persons, and Problems.* Phillipsburg, NJ: Presbyterian and Reformed, 1988.

Franke, Linda Bird. *The Ambivalence of Abortion.* New York: Dell Publishing Co., 1982.

Fryer, Peter. *The Birth Controllers.* New York: Stein and Day, 1965.

Fuller, O. E. *Brave Men and Women: Their Struggles, Failures, and Triumphs.* Chicago, IL: H. J. Smith and Co., 1887.

Furst, John K. L. *The English Journalistic Tradition.* London: Soughton Publishing House, 1966.

Gallagher, Hugh Gregory. *By Trust Betrayed: Patients, Physicians, and the License to Kill in the Third Reich.* New York: Henry Holt, 1990.

Garvey, John and Frank Morris. *Catholic Perspectives: Abortion.* Chicago: The Thomas More Press, 1979.

Gasman, Daniel. *The Scientific Origins of National Socialism.* London: MacDonald Publishing, 1971.

Gentry, Kenneth L. *The Christian Case Against Abortion.* Greenville, SC: Gentry PCA, 1982.

Glanze, Walter D. *The Signet/Mosby Medical Encyclopedia.* New York: Signet, 1987.

Glasow, Richard D. *School-Based Clinics, The Abortion Connection.* Washington, DC: National Right to Life, 1988.

Glessner, Thomas A. *Achieving an Abortion Free America by 2001.* Portland, OR: Multnomah Press, 1990.

Gordon, Linda. *Woman's Body, Woman's Right: Birth Control in America.* New York: Penguin Books, 1976.

Gorman, Michael J. *Abortion and the Early Church.* Downer's Grove, IL: InterVarsity Press, 1982.

Gould, Stephen J. *The Mismeasure of Man.* New York: Norton, 1981.

Grant, George. *Grand Illusions: The Legacy of Planned Parenthood.* Brentwood, TN: Wolgemuth & Hyatt, Publishers, Inc., 1988.

Grant, George. *Trial and Error: The American Civil Liberties Union and Its Impact on Your Family.* Brentwood, TN: Wolgemuth & Hyatt, Publishers, Inc., 1989.

Gray, Madeline. *Margaret Sanger: A Biography of the Champion of Birth Control.* New York: Richard Marek Publishers, 1979.

Green, Melody. *Children: Things We Throw Away.* Lindale, TX: Last Days Ministries, 1983.

Greere, Germaine. *Sex and Destiny: The Politics of Human Fertility.* New York: Harper and Row, 1985.

Griffin, Bryan F. *Panic Among the Philistines.* Chicago: Regnery Gateway, 1983.

Grosskurth, Phyllis. *Havelock Ellis: A Biography.* New York: Alfred A. Knopf, 1980.

Guhl, E., and W. Kroner. *Everyday Life of the Greeks and Romans.* New York: Crescent Books, 1989.

Guttmacher, Alan F. *Pregnancy, Birth, and Family Planning.* Revised and updated by Irwin H. Kaiser, M.D. New York: Signet, 1987.

Hafer, Dick. *I Know We're a Throw-Away Society . . . But This Is Ridiculous.* Glenn Dale, MD: Freedomlight, 1989.

Hamell, Patrick J. *Handbook of Patrology.* Staten Island, NY: Alba House, 1968.

Harakas, Emily. *Through the Year with the Church Fathers.* Minneapolis, MN: Light and Life Publishing, 1985.

Harakas, Stanley S. *Contemporary Moral Issues Facing the Orthodox Christian.* Minneapolis, MN: Light and Life Publishing, 1982.

Harper-Bill, Christopher. *The Pre-Reformation Church in England: 1400–1530.* London: Longman Press, 1989.

Harrison, Shelby M., and F. Emerson Andrews. *American Foundations for Social Welfare.* New York: Russell Sage Foundation, 1981.

Headland, Isaac Taylor. *Some By-Products of Missions.* New York: Jennings and Graham, 1912.

Hensley, Jeff Lane. *The Zero People: Essays on Life.* Ann Arbor, MI: Servant Books, 1983.

Hess, Rick and Jan. *A Full Quiver: Family Planning and the Lordship of Christ.* Brentwood, TN: Wolgemuth & Hyatt, Publishers, Inc., 1990.

Hilgers, Thomas W., Dennis J. Horan, and David Mall. *New Perspectives on Human Abortion.* Frederick, MD: Alethia Book, 1981.

Holm, Professor John James. *Holm's Race Assimilation.* Atlanta, GA: J. L. Nichols and Co., 1910.

Holmberg, Eric. *Pro-Life Rescues and Their Relationship to Spiritual Revival.* Gainesville, FL: Reel to Real Ministries, 1988.

Horman, Elisabeth. *After the Adoption.* Old Tappan, NJ: Revell, 1987.

Howard, Ted, and Jeremy Rifkin. *Who Should Play God?* New York: Dell Publishing, 1977.

Human Life International. *Banned Parenthood, Planned Barrenhood.* Gaithersburg, MD: Human Life International, 1988.

Humphrey, Derek. *Let Me Die Before I Wake: Hemlock's Book of Self-Deliverance for the Dying.* Los Angeles: Hemlock Grove, 1984.

Jaffe, Frederick S., Barbara L. Lindheim, and Philip R. Lee. *Abortion Politics: Private Morality and Public Policy.* Los Angeles: McGraw-Hill, 1981.

Johnson, Jean. *Natural Family Planning.* London: Catholic Truth Society, 1981.

Johnson, Paul. *Intellectuals.* New York: Harper and Row, 1988.

Johnson, Paul. *Modern Times: The World from the Twenties to the Eighties.* New York: Harper and Row, 1983.

Joinville and Vilehardouin. *Chronicles of the Crusades.* New York: Penguin Books, 1963.

Jones, Gareth D. *Brave New People: Ethical Issues at the Commencement of Life.* Downer's Grove, IL: InterVarsity Press, 1984.

Kasun, Jacqueline. *The War Against Population: The Economics and Ideology of Population Control.* San Francisco, CA: St. Ignatius Press, 1988.

Keeton, Kathy. *Woman of Tomorrow.* New York: St. Martin's Press, 1985.

Kennedy, D. James. *William Wilberforce: Christian Statesman.* Ft. Lauderdale, FL: Coral Ridge Ministries, 1982.

Kennedy, D. James with Norman R. Wise. *A Nation in Shame: Ample Evidence of America's Continuing Drift Toward Godlessness.* Fort Lauderdale, FL: Coral Ridge Ministries, 1987.

Kennedy, David M. *Birth Control in America: The Career of Margaret Sanger.* New York: Yale U Press, 1970.

Kevles, Daniel J. *In the Name of Eugenics.* London: Viking Books, 1986.

Kinsey, Alfred C., Wardell C. Pomeroy, and Clyde E. Martin. *Sexual Behavior in the Human Male*. New York: W. B. Saunders Co., 1948.

Klasen, Thomas G. *A Pro-Life Manifesto*. Westchester, IL: Crossway Books, 1988.

Kline, Meredith. *Treaty of the Great King: The Covenant Structure of Deuteronomy*. Grand Rapids, MI: Wm. B. Eerdman's Publishing Co., 1963.

Koop, C. Everett. *To Live or Die? Facing Decisions at the End of Life*. Ann Arbor, MI: Servant Books, 1987.

Koster, John P. *The Atheist Syndrome*. Brentwood, TN: Wolgemuth & Hyatt, Publishers, Inc., 1989.

Kowalczyk, John. *An Orthodox View of Abortion*. Minneapolis, MN: Light and Life Publishing Co., 1987.

Kreeft, Peter. *The Unaborted Socrates*. Downer's Grove, IL: Inter-Varsity Press, 1983.

Lane, Harold K. *Liberty! Cry Liberty!* Boston: Lamb and Lamb Tractarian Society, 1939.

Larue, Gerald A. *Euthanasia and Religion*. Los Angeles, CA: Hemlock Society, 1985.

Latourette, Kenneth Scott. *A History of Christianity*. New York: Harper Brothers, 1953.

Lester, Lane P. with James C. Hefley. *Cloning: Miracle or Menace*. Wheaton, IL: Tyndale House, 1980.

Lifton, Robert J. *The Nazi Doctors: Medical Killing and the Psychology of Genocide*. New York: Basic Books, 1986.

Lightfoot, J. B., and J. R. Harmer, eds. *The Apostolic Fathers*. Grand Rapids, MI: Baker Book House, 1989.

Lincoln, Abraham. *Speeches, Letters, and Papers: 1860–1864*. Washington, DC: Capitol Library, 1951.

Lindstrom, Paul D. *4 Days in May: Storming the Gates of Hell*. Arlington, IL: Christian Liberty Press, 1988.

Livingstone, David. *Missionary Travels and Researches in Southern Africa*. New York: England and Wilson Publishers, 1952.

Lucas, J. R. *Weeping in Ramah*. Westchester, IL: Crossway Books, 1985.

Luker, Kristin. *Abortion and the Politics of Motherhood*. Los Angeles, CA: University of California Press, 1984.

Macauley, Susan Schaeffer. *Something Beautiful from God*. Westchester, IL: Crossway Books, 1980.

MacCoby, S. *The Radical Tradition 1763–1914*. New York: University Press, 1957.

Macfie, A. L. *The Eastern Question: 1774–1923*. London: Longman Press, 1989.

Maddoux, Marlin. *Free Speech or Propaganda?: How the Media Distorts the Truth*. Nashville, TN: Thomas Nelson, 1990.

Maier, Pauline. *The Old Revolutionaries: Political Lives in the Age of Samuel Adams*. New York: Vintage Books, 1980.

Mains, Karen Burton. *Open Heart, Open Home*. New York: Signet, 1980.

Malherbe, Abraham J. *Moral Exhortation, A Greco-Roman Sourcebook*. Vol. 4 of *Library of Early Christianity*. Philadelphia, PA: The Westminster Press, 1986.

Marshall, Robert G. *Bayonets and Roses: Comprehensive Pro-Life Political Action Guide*. Washington, DC: Foundations for Life, 1976.

Marshner, Connie. *Decent Exposure: How to Teach Your Children About Sex*. Brentwood, TN: Wolgemuth & Hyatt, Publishers, Inc., 1988.

Marshner, William H. *The Right to Live*. Lynchburg, VA: Moral Majority, 1981.

Marx, Paul. *Confessions of a Pro-Life Missionary*. Gaithersburg, MD: Human Life International, 1978.

Mather, Cotton. *To Do Good: An Essay upon the Good That Is to Be Devised and Designed by Those Who Desire to Answer the Great End of Life and to Do Good While They Live*. Boston, MA: Sabbath School Society, 1845.

McCoy, Kathy. *The Teenage Body Book: A Guide to Sexuality*. New York: Simon and Schuster, 1983.

McDowell, Josh. *How to Help Your Child to Say "No" to Sexual Pressure*. Waco, TX: Word Books, 1987.

McDowell, Josh, and Dick Day. *Why Wait? What You Need to Know About the Teen Sexuality Crisis*. San Bernadino, CA: Here's Life Publishers, 1987.

McNeil, William H. *Plagues and Peoples*. London: Penguin Books, 1985.

Meeks, Wayne A., ed. *Library of Early Christianity*. 8 vols. Philadelphia, PA: Westminster Press, 1987.

Meeks, Wayne A. *The Moral World of the First Christians*. Vol. 6 of *Library of Early Christianity*. Philadelphia, PA: The Westminster Press, 1986.

Meltzer, Milton. *Rescue: The Story of How Gentiles Saved Jews in the Holocaust*. New York: Harper and Row, 1988.

Merton, Andrew H. *Enemies of Choice: The Right-to-Life Movement and Its Threat to Abortion*. Boston, MA: Beacon Press, 1981.

Mohr, James C. *Abortion in America*. New York: Oxford University Press, 1978.

Montgomery, John Warwick. *Slaughter of the Innocents*. Westchester, IL: Crossway Books, 1981.

Morris, Charles. *The Marvelous Record of the Closing Century*. Philadelphia, PA: American Book and Bible House, 1899.

Morse, Arthur D. *While Six Million Died: A Chronicle of American Apathy*. Woodstock, NY: The Overlook Press, 1983.

Mosbacker, Barrett L. *School-Based Clinics and Other Critical Issues in Public Education*. Westchester, IL: Crossway Books, 1987.

Muggeridge, Malcolm. *Something Beautiful for God: Mother Theresa of Calcutta*. San Francisco, CA: Harper and Row, 1971.

Nathanson, Bernard N. *Aborting America.* Garden City, NY: Doubleday, 1979.

Nathanson, Bernard N. *The Abortion Papers: Inside the Abortion Mentality.* New York: Frederick Fell, 1983.

Neill, Stephen. *A History of Christian Missions.* London: Penguin Books, 1964, 1987.

Nelson, Leonard J. *The Death Decision.* Ann Arbor, MI: Servant Books, 1984.

Newton, Richard. *Heroes of the Early Church.* Philadelphia, PA: The American Sunday School Union, 1888.

Nichols, Adrian O. P. *Holy Images.* London: Catholic Truth Society, 1987.

Nonkin, Lesley Jane. *I Wish My Parents Understood.* New York: Penguin Books, 1986.

North, Gary. *Trespassing for Dear Life: What Is Operation Rescue Up To?* Fort Worth, TX: Dominion Press, 1989.

North, Gary. *When Justice Is Aborted: Biblical Standards for Non-Violent Resistance.* Fort Worth, TX: Dominion Press, 1989.

Numbers, Ronald L. and Darrel W. Amundsen. *Caring and Curing: Health and Medicine in the Western Religious Traditions.* New York: Macmillan, 1986.

Olasky, Marvin. *Patterns of Corporate Philanthropy: Public Affairs Giving and the Forbes 100.* Washington, DC: Capitol Research Center, 1987.

Olasky, Marvin. *The Press and Abortion, 1838–1988.* Hillsdale, NJ: Lawrence Erlbaum Associates, 1988.

Olasky, Marvin and Susan. *More Than Kindness: A Compassionate Approach to Crisis Childbearing.* Westchester, IL: Crossway Books, 1990.

O'Neill, Nena and George. *Open Marriage: A New Style for Couples.* New York: Evans and Co., 1942.

Owen, Samuel A. *Letting God Plan Your Family.* Westchester, IL: Crossway Books, 1990.

Paine, Thomas. *Common Sense and Other Essays.* New York: Signet Classics, 1977.

Paul, Ron. *Abortion and Liberty.* Lake Jackson, TX: The Foundation for Rational Economics and Education, 1983.

Payne, Franklin E., Jr. *Biblical/Medical Ethics.* Milford, MI: Mott Media, 1985.

Perloff, James. *The Shadows of Power.* Belmont, MA: Western Islands, 1988.

Phan, Peter C. *Social Thought.* Wilmington, DE: Michael Glazier, Inc., 1984.

Pieper, Josef. *Leisure: The Basis of Culture.* New York: Mentor Books, 1952.

Planned Parenthood. *How to Talk with Your Child about Sexuality.* Garden City, NY: Doubleday and Co., 1986.

Plymouth Rock Foundation. *Biblical Principles: Concerning Issues of Importance to Godly Christians.* Plymouth, MA: Plymouth Rock Foundation, 1984.

Pollock, John. *A Fistful of Heroes: Great Reformers and Evangelists.* Grand Rapids, MI: Zondervan, 1988.

Pomeroy, Wardell. *Boys and Sex.* New York: Dell, 1981.

Pomeroy, Wardell. *Girls and Sex.* New York: Dell, 1981.

Powell, John. *Abortion: The Silent Holocaust.* Allen, TX: Argus Communications, 1981.

Prawn, Charles D. *The Bible and Birth Control.* Monongahela, PA: Zimmer Printing, 1989.

Prestige, G. L. *Fathers and Heretics.* London: SPCK, 1940.

Reagan, Ronald. *Abortion and the Conscience of a Nation.* Nashville, TN: Thomas Nelson, 1984.

Reardon, David C. *Aborted Women: Silent No More.* Westchester, IL: Crossway Books, 1987.

Riis, Jacob A. *The Making of an American.* New York: MacMillan, 1918.

210   BIBLIOGRAPHIC RESOURCES

Riis, Jacob. *Theodore Roosevelt: The Citizen*. London: MacMillan, 1912.

Rini, Suzanne M. *Beyond Abortion: A Chronicle of Fetal Experimentation*. Avon-by-the-Sea, NJ: Magnificat Press, 1988.

Roberts, Alexander, and James Donaldson, eds. *The Ante-Nicene Fathers*. 10 vols. Grand Rapids, MI: Wm. B. Eerdmans, 1983.

Rodman, Hyman, Susan H. Lewis, and Saralyn B. Griffith. *The Sexual Rights of Adolescents: Competence, Vulnerability and Parental Control*. New York: Columbia University, 1984.

Roosevelt, Theodore. *An Autobiography*. New York: Charles Scribner's Sons, 1926.

Roosevelt, Theodore. *Foes of Our Own Household*. New York: Charles Scribner's Sons, 1924.

Rothman, Barbara Katz. *The Tentative Pregnancy: Prenatal Diagnosis and the Future of Motherhood*. New York: Viking Penguin, 1986.

Ruff, Robert H. *Aborting Planned Parenthood*. Houston, TX: New Vision Press, 1988.

Rushdoony, Rousas John. *The Myth of Over-Population*. U.S.A.: Thoburn Press, 1969.

Ryle, J. C. *Christian Leaders of the Eighteenth Century*. Edinburgh, UK: Banner of Truth Trust, 1978.

Sanger, Margaret. *Margaret Sanger: An Autobiography*. New York: Dover Publishing, 1971.

Sanger, William. *The History of Prostitution*. New York: Eugenics Publishing Co., 1939.

Sassone, Robert L. *Handbook on Population*. 4th edition. Santa Ana, CA: R. L. Sassone, 1978.

Schaeffer, Francis A. *A Christian Manifesto*. Westchester, IL: Crossway Books, 1981.

Schaeffer, Francis, and C. Everett Koop, *Whatever Happened to the Human Race*. Old Tappan, NJ: Revell, 1980.

Schaeffer, Francis A., C. Everett Koop, Jim Buchfuehrer, and Franky Schaeffer V. *Plan for Action: An Action Alternative for Whatever Happened to the Human Race.* Old Tappan, NJ: Revell, 1980.

Schaeffer, Franky. *A Time for Anger: The Myth of Neutrality.* Westchester, IL: Crossway Books, 1982.

Schaeffer, Franky, and Harold Fickett. *A Modest Proposal: For Peace, Prosperity and Happiness.* Nashville, TN: Thomas Nelson, 1984.

Schaff, Philip. ed. *A Select Library of the Nicene and Post-Nicene Fathers of the Christian Church.* 14 vols. Grand Rapids, MI: Wm. B. Eerdmans, 1983.

Schaff, Philip, and Henry Wace, eds. *A Select Library of the Nicene and Post-Nicene Fathers of the Christian Church: Second Series.* 13 vols. Grand Rapids, MI: Wm. B. Eerdmans, 1983.

Scheidler, Joseph M. *Closed: 99 Ways to Stop Abortion.* Westchester, IL: Crossway Books, 1985.

Schlafly, Phyllis, ed. *Child Abuse in the Classroom.* Westchester, IL: Crossway Books, 1986.

Schlossberg, Herbert. *Idols for Destruction.* Nashville, TN: Thomas Nelson, 1983.

Seaman, Barbara. *The Doctor's Case Against the Pill.* Garden City, NY: Doubleday, 1980.

Shannon, Thomas A., and Jo Ann Manfra. *Law and Bioethics: Texts with Commentary on Major U.S. Court Decisions.* Ramsey, NJ: Paulist Press, 1982.

Shapiro, Howard I. *The Birth Control Book.* New York: Avon, 1977.

Sheils, W. J. *The English Reformation: 1530–1570.* London: Longman Press, 1989.

Shettles, Landrum, and David Rorvik. *Rites of Life: The Scientific Evidence for Life Before Birth.* Grand Rapids, MI: Zondervan, 1983.

Sider, Ronald J. *Completely Pro-Life*. Downer's Grove, IL: InterVarsity Press, 1987.

Sikorska, Grazyna. *Light and Life: Renewal in Poland*. Grand Rapids, MI: Zondervan, 1989.

Simon, John. *Paradigms Lost: Reflections on Literacy and Its Decline*. New York: Clarkson N. Potter, Inc., 1980.

Simon, Julian, and Herman Kahr, ed. *The Resourceful Earth: A Response to Global 2000*. Oxford, UK: Basil Blackwell, 1984.

Sjoo, Monica, and Barbara Mor. *The Great Cosmic Mother: Rediscovering the Religion of the Earth*. San Francisco, CA: Harper and Row, 1987.

Smith, F. LaGard. *When Choice Becomes God*. Eugene, OR: Harvest House, 1990.

Sobran, Joseph. *The Averted Gaze: Liberalism and Fetal Pain*. New York: The Human Life Foundation, 1984.

Sobran, Joseph. *Single Issues: Essays on the Crucial Social Questions*. New York: The Human Life Press, 1983.

Southern, R. W. *Western Society and the Church in the Middle Ages*. London: Pelican Books, 1970.

Spring, Beth, and Ed Larson. *Euthanasia*. Portland, OR: Multnomah, 1988.

Sproul, R. C. *Abortion: A Rational Look at an Emotional Issue*. Colorado Springs, CO: NavPress, 1990.

Sproul, R.C. *Lifeviews*. Old Tappan, NJ: Revell, 1986.

Spurgeon, Charles Haddon. *Spurgeon's Catechism*. Canton, GA: Word of Truth, 1979.

Stanbaugh, John E., and David L. Bolch. *The New Testament in Its Social Environment*. Philadelphia, PA: The Westminster Press, 1986.

Stanford, Susan M. *Will I Cry Tomorrow? Healing Post-Abortion Trauma*. Old Tappan, NJ: Revell, 1986.

Steele, Joel Dorman, and Esther Baker. *A Brief History of the United States*. Cincinatti, OH: American Book Co., 1900.

Stone, Abraham, and Norman E. Himes. *Planned Parenthood: A Practical Handbook of Birth Control Methods*. New York: Collier Books, 1965.

Stone, Hannah and Abraham. *A Marriage Manual*. New York: Simon and Schuster, 1968.

Stuckenbert, J. H. W. *The Age and the Church*. Hartford, CT: The Student Publishing Co., 1893.

Sutton, Ray. *That You May Prosper*. Fort Worth, TX: Dominion Press, 1987.

Swindoll, Charles R. *Sanctity of Life: The Inescapable Issue*. Dallas, TX: Word Publishing, 1990.

Tada, Joni Eareckson. *All God's Children: Ministry to the Disabled*. Grand Rapids, MI: Zondervan, 1987.

Television History Workshop. *Making History 5/ Birth Control*. London: Television History Centre, 1988.

Mother Teresa, Francis A. Schaeffer, et. al. *Who Is for Life?* Westchester, IL: Crossway, 1984.

Terry, Randall. *Accessory to Murder: The Enemies, Allies, and Accomplices to the Death of Our Culture*. Brentwood, TN: Wolgemuth & Hyatt, Publishers, Inc., 1989.

Terry, Randall. *Higher Laws*. Binghamton, NY: Project Life, 1988.

Terry, Randall. *Operation Rescue*. Springdale, CA: Whittaker House, 1988.

Toffler, Alvin. *Future Shock*. New York: Bantam Books, 1970.

Tracy, T. H. *The Seventh Commandment: Thirteen Cases of Divorce and Adultry*. New York: Abelard-Schuman, 1963.

Tucker, Ruth A. *Guardians of the Great Commission: The Story of Women in Modern Missions*. Grand Rapids, MI: Zondervan, 1988.

Tyrrell, R. Emmett, Jr. *Orthodoxy: The American Spectator Anniversary Anthology.* New York: Harper and Row, 1987.

Unger, Ken. *True Sexuality.* Wheaton, IL: Tyndale House, 1987.

U.S. Commission on Human Rights. *Hearing Before the United States Commission on Civil Rights: Protection of Handicapped Newborns.* Washington, DC: U.S. Printing Office, 1985.

Vertefeuille, John. *Sexual Chaos: The Personal and Social Consequences of the Sexual Revolution.* Westchester, IL: Crossway Books, 1988.

Veyn, Paul. *From Pagan Rome to Byzantium.* Vol. 1 of A History of a Private Life. Cambridge, MA: Belknap Press, 1987.

Walton, Rus. *One Nation Under God.* Nashville, TN: Thomas Nelson, 1987.

Ware, Timothy. *The Orthodox Church.* New York: Penguin Books, 1963.

Wattenberg, Ben J. *The Birth Dearth: What Happens When People in Free Countries Don't Have Enough Babies.* New York: Pharos Books, 1987.

Weiner, Roberta. *Teen Pregnancy: Impact on the Schools.* Alexandria, VA: Capitol Pub. Inc, 1987.

Weiss, Daniel Evan. *100 percent American.* New York: Poseidon Press, 1988.

Whitehead, John W. *Arresting Abortion: Practical Ways to Save Unborn Children.* Westchester, IL: Crossway Books, 1985.

Whitehead, John W. *The Separation Illusion.* Milford, MI: Mott Media, 1977.

Willke, Dr. and Mrs. J. C. *Abortion: Questions and Answers.* Cincinatti, OH: Hayes Pub. Co., 1985.

Willke, Dr. and Mrs. J. C. *Handbook on Abortion.* Cincinatti, OH: Hayes Pub. Co., 1979.

Willke, J. C. *Abortion and Slavery: History Repeats.* Cincinatti, OH: Hayes Pub. Co., 1984.

Wilson, A. N. *Hilaire Belloc.* London: Penguin Books, 1984.

Wilson, Ellen. *An Even Dozen.* New York: Human Life Press, 1981.

Wilson, Mercedes Arzu. *Love and Fertility: The Ovulation Method,* *The Natural Method for Planning Your Family.* New Orleans, LA: Family of the Americas, 1986.

Woiwode, Larry. *Born Brothers.* New York: Penguin Books, 1988.

Womer, W. L., ed. *Morality and Ethics in Early Christianity.* Philadelphia, PA: Fortress Press, 1987.

Young, Curt. *The Least of These.* Chicago: Moody Press, 1984.

SUBJECT INDEX

ABOUT THE AUTHOR

eorge Grant has been a leader in the pro-life movement as well as an advocate of the poor and homeless for more than a decade. He is a popular speaker and the prolific author of several books, including *Bringing in the Sheaves: Transforming Poverty into Productivity*, *Trial and Error: The American Civil Liberties Union and Its Impact on Your Family*, and the award winning exposè of the abortion industry, *Grand Illusions: The Legacy of Planned Parenthood*.

Mr. Grant is the Executive Director of Coral Ridge Ministries in Fort Lauderdale, Florida where he lives with his wife and three children. He is currently at work on a novel and a series of biographies.

The typeface for the text of this book is *Baskerville*. It's creator, John Baskerville (1706-1775), broke with tradition to reflect in his type the rounder, yet more sharply cut lettering of eighteenth-century stone inscriptions and copy books. The type foreshadows modern design in such novel characteristics as the increase in contrast between thick and thin strokes and the shifting of stress from the diagonal to the vertical strokes. Realizing that this new style of letter would be most effective if cleanly printed on smooth paper with genuinely black ink, he built his own presses, developed a method of hot pressing the printed sheet to a smooth, glossy finish, and experimented with special inks. However, Baskerville did not enter into general commercial use in England until 1923.

Substantive Editing:
Michael S. Hyatt

Copy Editing:
Cynthia Tripp

Cover Design:
Steve Diggs & Friends
Nashville, Tennessee

Page Composition:
Xerox Ventura Publisher
Printware 720 IQ Laser Printer

Printing and Binding:
Maple-Vail Book Manufacturing Group
York, Pennsylvania

Cover Printing:
Strine Printing
York, Pennsylvania